Stanley Victor Makower

The Mirror of Music

Stanley Victor Makower

The Mirror of Music

ISBN/EAN: 9783337085018

Printed in Europe, USA, Canada, Australia, Japan

Cover: Foto ©Thomas Meinert / pixelio.de

More available books at **www.hansebooks.com**

THE MIRROR OF MUSIC

A SMALL group of men sat round the fire of a club smoking-room. It was nearly two o'clock in the morning. There was no noise in the club, for every one else had gone home to bed. Outside the traffic had grown thinner. You could only occasionally hear the ringing sound of a hansom cab as it swung along the hard frosty street. Then all would be quiet again.

A heavy smell of cigars pervaded the room, and the smoke lay in thin layers at different levels in the air.

For nearly an hour the talk had been fragmentary—stray sentences exchanged between puffs of smoke. Now there was a general feeling that, unless something should arise to make the conversation particularly sociable and interesting, it was time to go to bed.

Just at this moment some one began to describe rather enthusiastically to his neighbour a woman whom he had met the night before. A difference of opinion soon arose between the speakers.

'The sort of woman who tells you everything at once—I know—rather intense, with short, dark hair, and dark, eager, stupid eyes—horrible.'

'Not at all horrible.'

'Short, dark hair and dark eyes—anything but that,' and, with a gesture of severe disapprobation, he threw the end of his cigar into the huge grate, where a small heap of coal burned brightly in yellow flames.

By this time the others began to interest themselves, and the conversation soon became general. Sides were taken and before long, by a kind of tacit agreement, each was in turn describing 'the only woman it was possible to like.'

This theme alone could have kept them together for five minutes longer; and it arose spontaneously, loosening their tongues like magic.

'I will give you my choice then—she must be fair and tall, with the eyes and hands of a Botticelli Madonna—eyes full of a great wisdom, and—and—'

He was interrupted by another who waved him off with impatient nods of the head.

'Yes, yes, but these fair women never have any character. Think of the greatest women—in the Bible—in history—the greatest French women—' He poured out a list of names helter-skelter, till the others burst into a loud laugh at the ridiculous jumble.

'Jeanne d'Arc,' he concluded, as if fired with a fresh inspiration, and, with an air of mock defiance on his face, 'she too was dark. It is absolutely certain.'

He was shouted down. The air rang with different names hurled at the speaker in reckless disregard of their bearing on the subject.

'Mary Magdalene!'

'Mary Stuart!'

'Marie Antoinette!'

'Marie Bashkirtseff!'

'Marie Lloyd!'

Peals of laughter and derision greeted each name as it was pronounced.

So the fun flashed from one to the other.

Two alone out of the group remained silent. One was a heavy, awkwardly built man who read nothing but science, but affected a love of literature. He was regarded by his companions as an interesting contribution to society, and at times indulged in a ponderous gaiety which was much appreciated.

He was puffing nervously at the stump of a cigar and shifting uneasily in his chair.

'Come now, your turn,' said some one.

Silence was proclaimed in order to give him time to gather his ideal woman into a convenient focus. The faces of the listeners wore a look of curious interest.

After a considerable pause a deep voice said very solemnly, 'She must be very small.'

A smile stole over the faces of his companions.

'*Parturiunt montes*,' muttered some one and a roar of laughter went round the room.

The heavy man smiled nervously and shifted still more uneasily. He did not understand the interruption, and it needed much apology and encouragement to induce him to continue.

'I think,' at last he said as solemnly as before, 'that her hair must be brown. At all events it must be dark.'

The admirers of the dark type of beauty chorused an approval.

'Brown eyes with plenty of light in them, and then,' he added slowly, as if coming with infinite effort to a great conclusion, 'she must dress very well.'

Laughter danced in the eyes of the listeners.

'A French woman?' asked some one.

'No—not a French woman.'

'A ballet-dancer?' said another tentatively, as if he feared he were going a little too far.

This time there was no reply, and there seemed to be a general feeling of disappointment that more fun had not been extracted from the last speaker.

The dull red coal in the grate fell together with a hollow, muffled sound. For a few moments there was silence.

There was still one among the group who had not spoken. Suddenly he was assailed.

'Severine, Severine,—of course,' everybody cried.

'It is your turn.'

'We cannot let you off.'

'You haven't amused us enough lately, and you will be leaving us soon without having told us one good thing. What is *your* opinion? Describe the woman who is your ideal.'

The man addressed shrugged his shoulders very slightly.

'I have no opinions,' he said. 'They are the property of the younger generation. I don't want to rob them of their rights.'

There was a curious ease about the way in which he spoke. It was impossible to detect a foreign accent, but there was an even rhythm in the pronunciation of the sentence that is not English, and his voice was soft and musical.

'To which generation do you belong then?'

'Will not this tell you?' he answered, as with his left hand he brushed from his forehead a lock of hair that had grown almost white. 'Besides, there is no ideal woman. Love? oh, yes. That is all very well—but you get tired of it, and, besides, it is often troublesome.'

Severine Maidanoff, the son of a wealthy Russian merchant, was born at Moscow in 1853. His mother died when he was quite a child, so that he could not even remember her face. At the university in his native town he quickly developed a taste for music and literature. He was just twenty-two when he was sent under brilliant auspices to Berlin to hold a nominal post there in the Embassy. Before he had been in the capital a year, it was intimated that it would be desirable for him to leave the country. He had studied official circles rather closely, and brought out a French novel called *La Femme de Berlin*, in which there were allusions to a lady in a high position. These were considered scandalous. He used to tell his young admirers that he was accordingly recommended 'to try a change of air.'

From Berlin he came to London, but had only stayed a few months when he was offered the Directorship of a large theatre in Moscow. He accepted and returned to his home, where he found his father dying. At his bedside was his eldest son, who was Severine's senior by six years, and had entered into his father's business.

On the death of old Maidanoff, who had amassed a fortune as a merchant, Severine came into plenty of money, which he spent in living well and travelling — chiefly between Moscow and Paris. In both these cities he was a perfectly familiar figure in the artistic world, partly owing to his novels which had achieved considerable success, and partly owing to the irresistible fascination of his personality.

In London the only version of his history that was known was his own; and the candid, irresponsible way in which he talked of himself secured him a pardon from many who would have condemned him if they had heard from other people what he himself told them.

He was now in London for one of those short periods when some musical or theatrical event claimed his attention. At the club, although he was at least forty, he was a centre of adoration among the young men, and they were determined not to let him off to-night without contributing his share to the conversation.

'Were you ever really in love?' suggested some one.

Severine looked up at the speaker—then gazing into the fire—

'I wonder,' he said meditatively. 'Have you ever heard of a musical composer called Kaftal?' he went on.

'Did he write a very modern kind of choral symphony?'

'Exactly.'

'They talked of reviving it in the papers.'

'Yes, that is why I have come to London for a while.' He flicked off a long head of ash into the fender.

'The composer was a woman,' he said quietly. 'Her name was Sarah Kaftal. . . . Sarah, Sarah,' he repeated to himself musingly.

'Perhaps you were in love with her?'

'I wonder.'

'Do tell us instead of wondering.'

'No, I don't think I have ever been what you would call "in love," but I could tell you something about her. She was a great musician.'

They began to grow interested: everybody thought he was going to tell, in his brilliant, fascinating way, some extraordinary experience in his life. They pulled their chairs closer to the fire.

Severine rose, dropped the end of his cigarette into the fireplace, and looked at his watch.

'Nearly three o'clock, I must go,' he said. And, as he spoke, he looked curiously at a picture that hung over the mantelpiece. It represented a club dinner party: all the members had risen, champagne glass in hand,

and were turning towards the chairman with an air of distinguished courtesy mixed with just a touch of boredom. Severine smiled faintly.

'I cannot tell you about Sarah Kaftal now,' he continued, 'it would take too long, . . . besides, I have a diary of hers at home. Anybody who cares to fetch it may read it, but he won't understand much about it: it is full of music.' And he left the room.

.   .   .   .   .

One evening a week later the same group of young men, with the exception of Severine Maidanoff, who had gone to Paris, assembled round the fire of the smoking-room. One of them had fetched the diary, which was neatly wrapped in white paper, and he was about to read it to his companions.

On the cover was written, in the elegant handwriting of Severine,

JOURNAL DE SARAH KAFTAL

A short genealogy of the Kaftal family, also in Severine's hand, was written on the flyleaf. The colour of the ink was fresh, and con-

THE MIRROR OF MUSIC

trasted strongly with the faded writing of the manuscript.

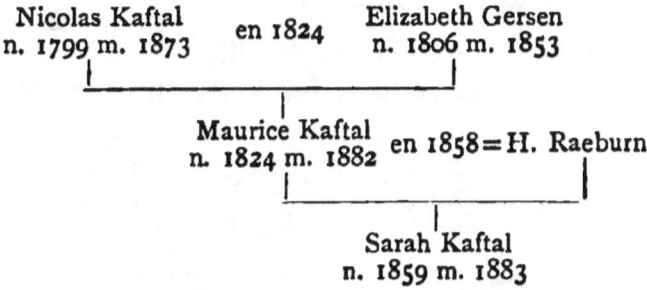

After glancing at the fly-leaf on which he made a few introductory comments, he read as follows :—

LONDON, 27*th October* 1879.

How blue the houses opposite look in the twilight—like fairy towers. The outlines are sharp and seem to suggest the forces of weight and gravitation more fully than when there is bright sunlight. A mist hangs round the chimneys in the square. It hardens into a clear atmosphere towards the centre. Through my window I can see the thin telegraph wires sloping delicately towards the mist in which they lose themselves. They seem to hang in the air without support.

It is getting darker. Shall I light the

candles and go on playing the *Appassionata* or ... no, I am tired. I will sit by the window and write till dinner-time.

What a wonderful thing this sonata is. I must have been at it for more than an hour.

Nearly black outside now, and it seems to suit my mood. There is something very mysterious about that melody, and the darkness seems part of it.

It is a perpetual worry to me not to know why I am so fond of music and what it is that fascinates me. For instance, what is there in that melody that is so great? The relations of the notes are not complicated: it is almost a commonplace air, yet Beethoven makes it colossal.

They are lighting up the houses opposite: one by one yellow flames peep out of the darkness. The noise of the traffic seems louder than when it was light. How the things roar:

one continuous note made up of rumbling carts and carriages. Sometimes I can hear a single cart rattle along at a higher note, and then gradually the sound is lost in the big roar. I wonder what note it is.

I have tried on the piano. It is

I must hurry to dinner—and my hair is so untidy, but I can't wait, and they must grumble as they always do at my appearance.

28th October.

They did grumble at my appearance. My mother said she did not know what would become of me, and that she was sure I should never be a happy wife because I was not tidy and domesticated. My father looked silently reproachful, and I sat uncomfortable all the evening. I could not eat anything. I never can, soon after playing. I went to bed and slept badly, waking frequently with the *Appassionata* ringing in my ears. This morning I am exhausted, I shall play a nocturne of Chopin, op. 62, No 2.

The opening melody is like a lily floating on clear water, and the middle like a swift undercurrent, muddy and weedy.

I don't know why, but I suddenly jumped up and ran to a long mirror on the wall, and stood gazing at myself for some time. How white my neck looked. I had never noticed it before. My mother found me in this position, and asked angrily what I was doing and why I was not ready to go shopping with her. I ran out, hastily put on my hat, and we left the house.

It was a lovely morning, soft and bright, and I enjoyed the cool air. My mother had a hundred and one purchases to make and I tried to be interested in them, but could never concentrate my attention, till at last she told me to wait outside as I only bothered her.

I sauntered to the Cork Street end of the Burlington Arcade, and then stood facing Piccadilly, while I watched the people walking up and down.

A tired feeling came over me as I stood there. From Piccadilly a broad stream of light entered the Arcade, and the people looked very pretty as they wandered from shop to shop. They were mostly ladies and their small heels clapped pleasantly on the paved way.

A mist came over my eyes. I seemed to see a whole picture—eternally moving. There was nothing more human about the figures, than about the windows, or the stone paving on which they walked. They were only part of a general scheme which seemed to be forming and reforming itself under my eyes. I fancied I could almost trace a pattern varying as they moved, but always harmonious. Schumann's *Arabesque* began to run through my head. Every figure seemed to do exactly its appropriate action.

A child, in a long white frock and hood, tottered from its mother's side to the toyshop on the other side of the Arcade. It seemed to flash across, but I felt instinctively that it too had filled a part in the scheme, and that if it had not moved in this direction I should have felt and known that something had gone wrong.

During luncheon I kept thinking of the crowd that I had watched and associating the movement of their feet on the pavement with

Minore 1.

29th October.

Nothing has happened to-day.

I am unhappy and discontented. I tried to do some needle work, and my mother was so pleased to see me away from the piano that she tried to show herself grateful by talking about music. She said it was one of God's best gifts, and that the music in church always made her feel spiritually exalted. I did not argue with her. What can be the meaning of this spiritual exaltation? Is it because we have always associated music with an afterlife, and sing hymns in church, that we have lost all idea of what the actual sounds really are, and so we subordinate them to the sense of the words? I always feel inclined to clap in church when they have sung something that pleases me.

But then I am very irreverent. I only go to church to please my mother. What should I, what can I believe? I who only have a dim consciousness of the people and things around me. They may be only phantoms created by my brain for all that I know. Any day they may vanish. Sometimes I feel as if they *were* vanishing, as if I were slipping away from them. But music is not a phantom—no, I am certain of that.

Sometimes as I have been walking dreamily along the streets, masses of people have hurried to and fro before my eyes, and I have passed on without feeling that they had any real existence. Then I have heard an organ begin to play, and a shudder has gone through me. The sound seems to symbolise a force of which man is but an offshoot, a by-product. I have felt a strange repulsion as if I had beheld the sun rise, throwing its golden beams on a corpse lying in a field naked. My mother has often told me that she, too, feels melancholy when she hears an organ in the street.

October 30*th.*

I think I am very beautiful. There is a harmony about me, a symmetry in the arrangement of line and colour which is satisfying to my eye. I do not think I have any vanity although I say this, for when I look at myself I admire a creation over which I seem to have no hold and in which I do not regard myself. I never grasp fully that my reflection in the glass and myself are inseparably connected.

I should like to go on the stage and sing, but it should be in an opera with no words. I would write the music, and it should have a deep meaning like the C minor symphony. Words cannot interpret, they can only mislead. Wagner's greatest triumphs were crying condemnations of his theories on art. When Tristan drinks the love potion there is music so intense, so maddening, that Tristan, Isolde, the gilt cup, and all the tawdry wings on the stage vanish from my sight. I cannot see them.

I was called away to pour out tea to a crowd of my mother's friends in the drawing-room. They asked me how I was progressing with my music, and said it must be so pleasant to be able to play when one was tired and wanted relaxation. I stared and said nothing, and my mother fearing a quarrel turned the conversation. Of the people I have met there is only one who does not talk of music in a way that is absolutely incomprehensible to me.

October 31*st.*

He has been much in my mind lately. He has very black hair, a thin sensitive profile, and very white hands. He is not tall. He is the son of a friend of my father's, a Russian, and he directs the chief theatre at Moscow. I remember hearing him play the violin when I was fourteen years old, and we were travelling in Russia on a visit to my grandfather who was dying. One evening when he was a little better we went round to the Maidanoffs', and Severine played the 'Kreutzer' Sonata. When he came to this:

I felt as if I had entered another world. I fainted in my mother's arms, and they said it was the heat of the room; but I remember distinctly that it was nothing of the kind.

It was a mild night in September. They had shut the windows to prevent the candle grease blowing about. The only two lights in the room were on the piano. We were in darkness in a corner. There was a plane-tree outside in the street, and a soft wind blew the dry leaves against the window-pane from time to time with a faint tapping sound.

Severine faced us: his head and shoulders in the full light of the candles, the lower part of his body in darkness. He stood in a magnificent attitude. His head was thrown back and his eyes glowed with the enthusiasm he caught from the music. I watched him for some minutes. His brother, who accompanied, played well, but I felt instinctively that a woman must play the piano part to make the performance perfect.

The magnificence of the music grew upon me. I was bewildered, and, when Severine came to the passage I have quoted, the head and shoulders seemed to rise, and their outline to become intenser. The colours of his face grew stronger, the blackness of his hair and

THE MIRROR OF MUSIC

the whiteness of his skin terrified me, and the eyes were thrown up, following the bow with a strange inhuman light in them. Just at this moment the wind blew the leaves of the tree outside violently against the casement. The sudden noise must have dispelled the picture which my imagination had created. All at once I became conscious of my surroundings, and then I fainted.

I saw Severine a few years afterwards in London, and we talked about the 'Kreutzer.' Then he went away to Russia, and I have not seen him since. I asked about him the other day, and my father looked grave and said I was not to mention his name at home. I suspected there had been some scandal, and found out afterwards, that he had seduced the daughter of a general of high standing in the Russian army. There had been a duel in which both parties had been wounded, Severine only slightly, but his antagonist seriously. They said that if he lived he would be an invalid all his life. A sad story—that touched me deeply, and yet somehow I could not feel angry with Severine, though I tried very hard.

How cruel of him! I drew a sentimental

picture of the girl he had betrayed. She must be young and fair with Heine's 'liebes-kranken Augen.' And now she was ruined — had nothing to look forward to but — I shuddered: yet, as soon as I thought of Severine, my view of the tragedy was changed. It seemed to me to be only God fulfilling himself in many ways, and I could only treat it as a phenomenon; like a leaf borne on the surface of a stream. The stream symbolised to me the eternal undeviating course of the world, and the music of Schumann came into my head:

I have always felt that most of the intelligible meaning which has been attached to music is a false one—the mere result of association. The only meaning it can have is a sensual one. Yet even if this is so, why should we think that this meaning is wicked because it is sensual? And yet—

I have been thinking of Wagner again.

How blind he seems to be to the essential features of his own genius. His greatest triumphs are—what? Embodiments of an abstract emotion. But he has shown me that music can sometimes suggest things. The fire-motif in *The Walküre*, what of that? There is all the sensation of real fire about it: the steaming vapour, the tongues of flame. Again, in the opening of *Tristan*, the steersman's song of 'Frisch weht der Wind.' There is wind and sea breeze. And the Rhine music? Water.

Fire, Wind, Water; all unmistakable.

When I think of the images that music has sometimes suggested to me, I find they are all images of natural phenomena, by which I mean to exclude entirely the suggestion of men and women. As I write, Mozart's aria, 'Dove Sono,' in the *Nozze di Figaro*, is running through my head. When I hear it, I think of a sunbeam on a green field after rain. But, when I first heard it, I was only conscious of being moved in a very exquisite way. Afterwards it struck me that I was moved in much the same way when I saw a sunbeam on a green field after rain. Since then, I have connected the two things. If I see one, I hear the other. If I hear one, I see the other. But the sound seems to contain the picture, while the picture does not contain the sound.

Most music does not suggest any image to me because it gives me new sensations, such as no things I have ever seen have produced upon me. This is particularly the case with Beethoven, and I cannot find in him a single clue to my admiration, for he does not suggest even himself.

All this afternoon I have been thinking again about the origin of music. What else am I to do here? It is so dull—so unspeakably dull. The people who come are so ugly and stupid, and they hate me because I don't talk to them.

November 2nd.

I have searched through the poets to find some true insight into music, but they nearly all talk of it in connection with the soul, either vaguely or in a way that is misleading. I suppose none of them divine the truth that music expresses, but Shelley comes nearest.

November 3rd.

It is growing cold. Of late, I have neglected

the piano, and have been turning over the leaves of my diary, wondering how it will all end. I cannot play Chopin in the winter with a fire in my room. I like to play him when the air is hot and heavy with the scent of lime. The music I love best I play in the summer, and I spend the winter more in studying, than enjoying the things I play. But Beethoven is for all seasons of the year.

I intend to begin practising hard now. I told my father yesterday that I should like to become a professional musician. He looked strangely at me, and said I was not to think of it. I felt vexed and disappointed, then sullen, and now we do not talk together much.

November 10th, 11 p.m.

Yesterday I stole off to a concert by myself in the afternoon. They played the C minor symphony. I shut my eyes and listened to every note. When it was over, the applause sounded like rushing water in my ears. I looked up and saw a blurred mass of faces, but I looked at them for a long time without knowing what they were. And then a strange feeling came over me when I remembered that I was one like them with a face and hands.

I am writing an opera. Why I call it an opera I don't know, for there will be no words and no scenery.

I have to lock myself in my room for fear my mother should come in and find out what I am doing. I tell her that the servants so constantly interrupt my reading, that I am obliged to shut them out. A weak lie!

How I hate it all, and there is something so sad about it—I should have liked to make a confidante of my mother, to have told her everything, and asked her advice, but it is useless. I think she is disappointed in me. She would have liked a daughter who would have helped her in her house and gone out with her into society, both of which I have always resolutely refused to do. Sometimes I fancy that my mother has shuddered when I have kissed her before going to bed. She has seemed to have a physical repugnance to touching me. My father is very kind, but we do not understand each other. He has no taste for music. It bores him. So I live alone—quite alone. I had school friends, but they are all married and I don't like their husbands, so I never visit them.

Why don't I get married? This is what worries my parents, I am sure. The house is often full of men, but I can never talk to them. They are all the same, I hate the sight of them, and they try to be so obliging! Yet I am getting weary of living alone like this. I should like to go into the world and see what men really are, and what they think about. I feel as if I were being mocked and cheated in this respectable cage where there is no life, but everything is reduced to the level of a humdrum comfort. I should like to sing to large audiences. My voice should make people faint just as I fainted when Severine—

How his face haunts me. I never can think of him without seeing that strange look—the head thrown back—the eyes with an inhuman light in them.

I fancy I saw a shadow of a head and shoulders on the wall just now. Only fancy,

I am sure, but the candle light reminds me of Moscow.

I am cold. I must go to bed.

November 15*th.*

I have practised hard and written a good deal of my opera. I feel better, and I have come to a new determination. I shall change my habits and go out more. What is the good of trying to live alone without a soul to talk to? And my music often exhausts me so much that I can't go on. I told my mother yesterday that I would go to a dance at the Lorrimers', for which I had received an invitation. She received my decision with a look of astonishment which she tried in vain to disguise, but I could see that she was pleased, and I would have liked to rush into her arms and kiss her —only—

I am quite surprised myself at this new development, and not a little curious to know where it will lead me. I spent hours this morning trying to think of what dress I could wear for the ball. Till now I have insisted on dressing in black with scarcely any relief. This, too, has offended my mother, who loves plenty of colour, and thinks that my choice of black is a criticism on her own taste.

I tried many combinations in my mind, the last (which I think I shall have) is to be like this: I will have a soft silk, *eau de Nil* colour, with a high empire waist and a loose girdle embroidered in silver thread. My neck and shoulders shall be bare, and I will have two turquoise blue velvet bows tied under my arms, which shall stand up on my shoulders. I will wear no jewels, and there shall be no trimming to my dress but this: a trail of long drooping white roses coming across my right shoulder down to the left side of the skirt.

I am writing like a book of fashions—never mind; I think I shall look beautiful if they carry out my directions.

I am not quite sure that, when the time comes, I shall not feel alarmed at all this magnificence and refuse to go. At all events, till it does come, I shall have something to think about beside the Pathetic Sonata and my opera.

November 23*rd*.

Nothing new, but I want to write. I may as well describe my opera.

It includes images of trees of all colours and flowers of all shapes and smells, and rivers of all paces. And there are sun, stars, light, darkness. The rest I understand perfectly, but cannot set down. It will be quite intelligible to musicians, who will not try to associate actual objects with the music.

There is a chorus of men and women, and they sing, but they do not act. They are treated purely as an instrument.

Of course there are no words; but I have arranged and selected a number of sounds for them to use: a 'song' language, in the making of which I have taken trouble. It is often difficult to hit upon the appropriate sound for a note, but I make each member of the chorus sing to me alone, using such sounds or fictitious words as may suggest itself to him in a particular passage. As a rule, I can see a principle running through them all. This 'song' language is simple on the whole. It consists chiefly of liquid consonants and different vowel sounds. To make the people who sing fall in love with one another would be just as false as to make the violin fall in love with the flute. When they sound together they express a sort of completion, nothing more. So it is with my human voices.

I have often felt while walking in the streets as if the objects around me were only illustrations of some ideal object which we cannot see: a queer uneasy feeling as if we had sunbeams and were for ever vainly struggling to see the sun. So I have often felt that the life in a crowd of people is a feeble flickering thing—as it were—an imperfect impression only of the universal life dimly reflected in a mirror.

Words, action, and scenery are like restless shadows of humanity to me. I am always groping after the substance which seems to lie concealed behind them. So, when associated with music they only clog my appreciation of the truth which the sounds express directly and simply. But, then, there is no opera in which the libretto and the scenery are in themselves artistic enough to convey truths; so that I can think of no example to prove that even under these conditions, the combination would be a wrong one; yet it seems to me improbable that the separate portions, of which each art, in itself perfect, might be composed, should fit one another when brought together, and unless this is so, must not the three things, music, words and scenery, remain independent throughout as they actually do in Wagner? This would be more obvious in his operas, if his libretti were not so full of gods, demigods, and other conveniences by which he seeks to make faint the border-line between the rationalism of the dialogue and the mysticism of the music. In this he shows a marvellous cunning, but where he tries to be purely human in the dialogue the falseness shows through.

Here and there we catch a faint gleam of truth, but on the whole such passages are meaningless: the music meaningless without the words, powerless to interpret when combined with the words.

But why do I seek proof for what I know to be true? Do I not feel that music illustrates its ideal more clearly to me than either poetry and painting can illustrate theirs? This is reason enough for my reluctance to combine the three, and in this lies the secret of Wagner's mistake; for he is never a poet and never a painter, though he thinks he is both; but he is always a musician, and I cannot think of any musician who was either poet or painter.

Enough for to-day. There is a feeling of snow in the air.

December 2nd.

The snow did not come till to-day, but now it is slipping down in large white flakes. There is a hush over all the earth, which is covered with a hard whiteness.

The roar of the traffic has ceased. Every now and then I can hear from my room the sound of a cart or carriage as it slushes through a mound of snow, but it corresponds to no note on the piano.

This evening I am going to the Lorrimer's. My dress has come, and I have not yet had the curiosity to look at it. Perhaps it won't fit. Then I shan't go at all—well.

I am ready now and waiting for my mother. My dress does fit perfectly, and I looked at myself with great pleasure in the glass. For some moments I stood gazing at the shape and colour of the blue velvet bows that I was arranging. I became absorbed in trying to bring them into proper relation with the rest of the picture that I saw in the glass. First they were too stiff, then too flat. I began humming a fugue of Bach. The bows were obstinate: they would not crumple into the folds that I wanted. Now I crushed them, now stiffened them, and all the time I hummed the fugue right through. When I came to the last bar, which I hummed *rallentando*, a light pat just before the final note set them right.

December 3rd.

I am very tired to-day, but yesterday was a great success. I danced every dance. Though I always feel giddy and the lights whirl round, I never fall. But I have an intoxicating sensation. Once yesterday I thought that I was valsing on the top of a globe and that the people fell away in circles below me. I seemed to make no progress, but to whirl round always on the same point. And it seemed as if there were nothing overhead and around but space—a diaphanous whiteness which made the eyes tingle. The movement of my feet was quite without effort. They seemed to go without any direction, and I felt as if the whole weight of my body had been taken away. But when we stopped, all the colours of the room rushed upon my eyes, and I felt dazzled and strange. While I was valsing I had not been conscious of the temperature, but now the room seemed hot and confined. Where I had danced white rose-leaves had fallen. I traced the pattern which they made and found that I must have danced in gradually decreasing circles. Perhaps this accounts for the sensation I described above.

During the intervals between the dances, I looked at the people in the room. The men evidently noticed me intently. The women watched me closely, but there was an affectation of indifference about their glances, and I fancied that some of them looked angry. My mother alone wore a look of unclouded pleasure. She was prettily dressed in black and mauve, and it struck me as pathetic that on this occasion we had changed tastes.

I tried to remember this morning what my partners had said to me, but I could not think of a single remark they had made. I suppose I can't have listened to what they said.

There was a large oval mirror set in a gilt frame at one end of the room. It was interesting to watch the reflections of the people dancing. Once when I started from the other end of the room my eye caught a figure in the glass that fascinated me. This time we danced straight down the room, and the faces of the people did not become all blurred and indistinct as they do when I dance in a circle. Not till I was close up to the glass did I discover that the figure was myself. We stopped opposite the looking-glass and instinctively I lifted my arm to my head to see if the figure in the glass would do the same.

It did do the same, and relieved me of a queer, uneasy feeling that I was haunted by a shadow.

I always dance to the rhythm of the valse, but the melody seems in the way. The bars that suit me best are those in which the bass indicates the beat before the melody commences.

The valses of Strauss, the Hungarian valses of Brahms, the valses of Chopin, are all

THE MIRROR OF MUSIC

exquisite on the piano, but I don't want to dance while I am listening to them. I can imagine a sort of parallel scheme of poses that might be beautiful, but the valse would have to be forsaken for a less regular movement.

The snow was falling as we left in the early morning. A flake fell on my shoulder as we were stepping into the carriage. It felt soft and warm, but the air was biting and it was very dark. As we drove along, the scene of the ball-room was before my eyes. It hung in the black air before me like an unframed picture. A bright soft light fell from it, the colours of the dresses were delicate, and on the polished floor was the pattern of white rose-leaves that had fallen from my dress.

December 20*th.*

A whole fortnight since the ball, and I am growing dull and depressed again.

I have been thinking of my childhood. I cannot remember many definite occurrences, but I remember the sort of vague, dreamy way in which I looked at everything. My favourite remark was 'I don't understand,' for which I never failed to be called either 'excessively stupid,' or 'excessively obstinate.' So I used to grow more and more unhappy. It was so hard not to be able to understand things, and then to be laughed at or punished as well; yes, over and over again, I would be punished for what I could not possibly help, and my real sins, which were plentiful enough, were passed over in silence. I remember one particular instance.

It was the day before I went to my first school; I had been wilful and disobedient and refused to work with my governess. I was ill-disposed and out of humour. I was then eight years old. I argued with my governess. Everything seemed so ugly that day. In the course of the argument, I said firmly, and with some conviction in my voice, that I was unhappy and that no amount of luxury and education could make up for that. Miss Hughes looked surprised, and soon a stern look came into her eyes. But I repeated all that I had said. It was the one thing that I really knew, and I was determined not to compromise. All the concession that I made was to say that, 'as circumstances were' (I remember the feeling of superiority with which

I used this phrase), I should not run away, but, if things became worse I would go and be a flower girl. Miss Hughes saw that it would do no good to reason with me, so I was left alone until my father came home in the evening. There was a great deal of whispering in the house, and I crept about waiting for something to happen. Then my father came to me and asked how my lessons had been that day. With a tremendous effort I confessed that I had been lazy and disobedient.

'Yes, and something else besides,' he said, looking meaningly at me.

I puzzled for a moment helplessly. Then he grew angry. 'You said you were unhappy,' he said.

I was bewildered. I had confessed what seemed to be my real sin: here was an imaginary one set up as the chief. But he looked at me with a mysterious air of rebuke and sent me upstairs for a week. During that week, I tried very hard to imagine how wicked I was, but I could not conceive that it was a sin to say I was unhappy. I had made no reproaches to any one for contributing to my unhappiness. I was simply miserable and that was all. But every one looked askance at me. I was treated as an outcast for that week.

I wish there were more dances. I don't care for the theatres, for I always feel that my place is on the stage and not among the audience.

Severine has been in my mind again lately. I have been wondering if I shall ever see him. This morning I wandered through the Kreutzer and imagined the violin parts.

I have been thinking that the audience must be in complete darkness when my music is performed. They must not be able to see anything at all. They must only hear.

I think it shall be called an operatic symphony: for, though it is a protest against opera, it will contain operatic feeling, while the form will, with modifications, be that of a symphony. It is only the scenic and dramatic parts of operas that are wrong. When these are the leading motives the music suffers, but I think there is enough pure music in Wagner, in spite of his theories, to justify me in using operatic methods.

How cold it is, I can scarcely hold the pen, my fingers are so numb.

The night is clear, with blinking stars and a pale moon. I fancy that they are notes of some great instrument, and that if they were touched they would sound. Star music! I love to look at them and trace patterns in the sky. Just now I saw a splendid curve that reminded me of the trail of roses that I wore in my dress at the Lorrimers'. I feel as if I should like to go out and wander through the streets. I wonder whether they would hear me if I slipped out very quietly.

I have opened the window. How splendid the air feels upon my skin. I must go out. It will be so glorious to walk in the night with the cold stars overhead, and the glistening white snow on the ground.

Not a gleam of white in the sky, and I have managed to creep in without disturbing anybody. I scarcely know whether it has been a dream or whether—

But there is a reality in the cold that seems to have pierced every fibre in my body. I shall light a fire and try to put down all that I have experienced. I cannot go to bed for there is no sleep in my eyes.

For two hours I must have wandered without consciously taking any direction. The streets through which I walked were very quiet, and the snow on the pavement stopped any noise that my feet might have made. I half closed my eyes as I wandered, and felt the cold air blowing my hair about my forehead.

Gradually I began to think that the city in which I was walking was a creation of my brain. There were tall grey spires and soft yellow lights, but no people, and a dead hush all around. Occasionally a figure passed, but it seemed to belong to my imaginary city, and to have no life. Softly it slipped past me, and was lost in the darkness. Although my feet were going on, I felt as if I were stationary, and the houses were moving.

A deep note seemed to sound from the stars. It went down in a chromatic scale, and then ascended at the same intervals. The notes were very long, and awoke faintly the other sounds in the dominant major chord. I had never heard music so intense.

Soon I did not recognise that the things I passed were houses at all. They were masses of colour, and every now and then they formed beautiful patterns. So they flitted past me, and all I could feel was a strange wonder and the tingling of the sounds that beat upon me.

Then, gradually, these sounds grew less intense, and I had a dim consciousness of flowing water. It grew and grew, and I began to hear a melody from it:—

A rushing passionate sound as of a strong under-current.

I came to a broad open place brilliantly lighted. It was the Embankment. I heard the water mingling with the melody, which I remember now is Schumann's.

The imaginary city began to fade before the real one. I saw a boat glide along the water which glimmered with golden patches, and I could hear the noise of the keel as it grated against masses of floating ice. And then close to me black and hard, like mosaic on the snow, I saw the shadow of leafless trees.

A hot aching feeling came into my feet. I dragged along wearily until I found myself at Piccadilly Circus. There were a few carriages about. Most of the people from the theatres must have gone home, but there were lots of men on the pavement, and strange looking women, some of them very beautiful. I leaned against a lamp-post, and almost sank in the snow from exhaustion. But I watched the people round me, and felt a savage satisfaction in being in the midst of them, not shut up at home in a cage. Some one spoke to me. I did not answer, but crept away—I thought of the girl Severine had seduced, and felt the same difficulty in condemning him as before.

Here it was like a scene out of an opera. I should not have been surprised at anything. I felt as if all the people were actors on a stage.

Flakes fell on my face. I looked up. The sky was black—no stars were to be seen, and it had begun to snow. There was a melting of the crowd. The men and the beautiful women with the glistening eyes slipped away.

Swiftly I stole along with a feeling of numb warmth in me till I reached the house. Then

I crept up the steps, gently turned the latch-key, and climbed upstairs.

I cannot close my eyes now. They feel stiff and hard. The fire flickers, the yellow flashes frighten me. Severine's head and shoulders are there again. I wish I could forget him.

How that star-music rings in my ears. It was not the sound of a bow drawn across a string, but rather the sound of a glass rubbed on the brim with a moist finger, intensified a million times. Ah! It was splendid to be out in the cold, clear air, and to feel free.

I am trying to remember some of the patterns and colours that I saw, but they are all gone.

I am gradually thawing, and a drowsy feeling is coming over me. I think I shall go to bed.

February 14th.

What a long time since that wonderful night. How ill I must have been. For a week I was unconscious, sometimes delirious. I raved about the stars, they told me. Perhaps not so much raving as they imagined. But it all seems so far away now, and I am not sure in my own mind whether I really did go out, or whether I stayed at home and imagined all the experiences I put down in my diary. But if I did not go out, how can I account for my sudden illness?

I am very weak—I can only just write, and they have forbidden me to do it, but I snatch at the desk which lies close to me, as soon as they leave me alone, and write.

February 16*th.*

I asked them to let me hear some one play the piano, but they told me gently, but I could see firmly, that at present I must keep quiet and not think of hearing music.

My mother has been an angel to me during my illness. She has never left my bedside, and she has humoured all my whims. Yesterday, she brought me a bunch of white Narcissus, and arranged them just as I love to see them in a tall white glass. I think that we really have a great love for each other. Perhaps, if we had not, our differences of taste would not be so painful. I see my father so rarely, and he is so reserved when he is with me, that I do not know what he is like; but he has no taste for music, and he tries to discourage me as much as possible,

THE MIRROR OF MUSIC

from making it an absorbing pursuit. I have never asked him why he has such a rooted aversion to it. I feel somehow that his dislike is instinctive, that it is associated with something too near him to be revealed or touched upon.

February 17*th.*

I am advancing rapidly now. The doctors say that I must have done something very rash to catch such a chill. I only smile faintly. I dare not tell them what I did, or they will think me mad, and I want to spare my mother.

It is milder than it was. The snow has all gone, and there is a bright blue sky to-day with large white clouds hurrying over it. I want to go out. It is so dull to be in bed. I want to play again. I hear no music but the street whistles that float in through my window.

The doctor has called again. What a bore he is with his inevitable smile, and his long coat, but he has given me permission to get up to-morrow for a while.

I wish they would take away the vase of Narcissus. They are withered and dry. There is too much suggestion of corruption about them.

I dreamed last night that I was a large white

lily in a wood full of firs. I could feel my head shake on the stem when the wind caught me. I could hear the faint whispering of the firs as they trembled, but I could not see. Then I heard footsteps, and something sharp was cut into the stem and I was borne off—my head nodding dreamily.

Then I began to feel that I was losing my vigour, that my skin was growing dry and hard and that I was shrivelling up, and I knew that I should die.

But I woke before I had time to die—it was all the fault of those heads of white Narcissus. They should be taken away.

February 18*th.*

I have been thinking of Severine again. I want to see him more than ever. I cannot recollect how he really looks. I have only in my mind a very vivid picture of him on that night in Moscow as he was painted by my excited imagination. I cannot dissociate him from the head and shoulders with the inhuman light in the eyes. They are magnified still further now. The size is colossal, like some stone image of a sphinx. I cannot see the eyes, but only hollow caverns with a great light shooting from them.

February 26th.

They have ordered me to the sea in a day or two, so that I may gain strength. I want to go on with my composition, but they won't let me do any work, and I have not time while they are out of the room to put anything down but a few scraps of melodies on slips of paper.

I was quite contented when I was recovering from my illness. I could not think of anything, or move, but I had just sufficient consciousness to feel the physical joy of existence. Now that I am well and walk about again, the old troubles are beginning to seize me.

They have taken up the straw that was laid down in the square, so that I can hear the traffic again. I did not know before that they had put down this straw. I thought it was all quiet because the ground was covered with snow, and I kept thinking of my silent walk on that cold night.

Now I can hear the rattle of the wheels again, and I am trying to fix the note in my head. And then I begin wondering what gives the note its peculiar meaning to me. But my head aches. No more for to-day.

February 28th.

To-morrow I am to go to the sea-side with my mother. I hope we shall not stay very long, for I want to be back so that I can work hard. But it will be splendid to hear the roar of the sea and to feel the salt air on my skin. I feel better and my head is stronger. I don't dream so much at night. But I want to play. Oh, I do want to play. They have promised to let me begin again in a week. They know it is no good forbidding me for longer.

BOURNEMOUTH, *February 29th.*

Besides the sea, there is country; woods of fir-trees quite close to us. The sea is very calm to-day. It looks like a solid stretch of asphalt. I should not be surprised to see somebody walk across it quite securely. It is not at all beautiful. But the wind is fine, not very high but fresh and light. It blew the ribbons of my hat in front of me as I walked this morning; I threw back my head to prevent my hat being blown off, and then breathed in the fresh air. I am told to be in before the sun sets, but I shall try and stay out if I can escape my mother's vigilance.

She is pleased and contented with me on the whole. I have done a little needlework to propitiate her and make her receive the sin that I am going to commit in a spirit of greater resignation.

I have seen the sun set and it was splendid. Starting from the east end I walked along the shore of the bay. The horizon was before me in a complete unbroken semi-circle. As I walked it grew darker, and the sun turned to a sullen crimson colour. I went on for a few minutes, then looked back. A section of the semi-circle was covered with a grey mist out of which golden specks seemed to tingle. Then I walked on again and stopped once more and looked behind me. The grey mist had crept over another section. When I reached the pavilion on the pier, all on my left was covered in the mist. I faced the sea and looked each side of the pavilion. On the right the sun was sinking fast. It had turned a pale yellow colour, and soft beams shot upwards from it. On the left was the grey mist that had crept over half the semi-circle. Behind me was the town: black and mysterious, with yellow lights flickering here and there. Then I walked to the end of the bay, and the mist crept after me until I was in the last narrow section of the semi-circle, and saw the dying sun struggling through a dull white cloud.

One more moment and he was gone, and the mist was over all the horizon, and the tingling gold specks had vanished from it. A light breeze sprang up. I shuddered with the cold, and hurried home.

My mother was in terror at my rash conduct. I was in no mood for discussing the question, so retired sullenly to my room where I sat for some time in front of the fire that they had lighted for me, thinking over the scene that I had just witnessed. There was something in it that alarmed me. I felt an unaccountable fear that this creeping mist was somehow associated with me in a foreboding way, but I could see no definite application, so I gave up thinking about it.

March 4th.

We have been here a week now, and I shall be glad to go home again. This place tires me. There is nothing interesting in it. It is too cold to sit in the pine-woods, and there is nothing to do but listen to the roar of the sea which has turned angry enough ever since the night when I saw the sun set.

To morrow we return to London and then I am to be restored to my piano.

LONDON, 5*th March.*

At last. How refreshing London is to me. The almond-trees are beginning to blossom. Spring is coming. I can feel it. This one hour at home has done me more good than all the time at the sea. I have played the piano already, at first listlessly, but after I had touched a few chords, I flew off into the Pathetic and played it right through. I had never understood until now the meaning of this—

but it overwhelmed me this time as I played it. It is like the world forming itself out of chaos. Certainly there is more than this one planet in it.

I am horribly out of practice. My hands stick. But they will soon grow supple again. It will not take me long.

My work goes on. I should advance more rapidly with it if I did not continually sit and wonder what the material is from which I am making a selection. I can only feel its existence, but I cannot trace it home to any object or phenomenon that is round me. I can only make wild guesses which perplex me further.

I am beginning really to understand the Pathetic. There are still passages in it which I do not feel, but I am certain that if I go on studying, something will come out of them. My intellect does not help me in the least, except in so far as it is a medium through which to pass to the sensual appreciation. Just as a minute description of a dying man might not affect me at all; but once in his presence, I should understand what the situation was, and it would not be possible for me to do so unless

I knew first intellectually what was at stake and what was the material of the situation.

6th March.

My father is less reserved than usual. I think he is glad to see me well again. He asked me this morning how long I meant to practise a day, and I answered ambiguously. He was dissatisfied, but not angry. Why he is so averse to my indulging my favourite passion, I cannot think. If I only had the courage I would ask him some day for an explanation. But he looks so cold.

I feel that the spring is beginning. Yes, there are actually tiny little green shoots in the trees in our square, and there is a softness in the air that cannot be mistaken. I am watching with great interest the growth of the crocuses in the flower-boxes on the windows of the opposite houses. Every morning the tiny yellow heads increase. They look like little flames from my window.

The dusty smell of the streets is mingled with the perfume of flowers on trucks. How beautiful is the feeling of another summer coming upon us. I shall gradually change my répertoire. It is not hot enough yet for Chopin, but I shall play Schumann in his more classical moods. I must reserve the songs for May.

I find my composition gradually changes as the spring comes on. There will certainly be something in my work parallel to the seasons of the year. More than that I must not say.

14th March.

My birthday, and they have insisted on asking a number of relations to dinner to congratulate me on not having died before the age of twenty-one. I should have mortally offended my mother if as I at first intended I had resolutely refused to *fête* this uninteresting occasion. I have never been grateful for being born. It is a sentiment that I cannot grasp, and perhaps my mother would have felt my refusal as an unkind protest. Yet these ceremonies seem to me to accentuate the loneliness of each of us at home. For we are lonely, each isolated from the other, and we live side by side, and we cannot touch each other. My father is busy all day long with science. It is his only occupation. He has not a large practice, but he is trying to find a cure for some disease. Nearly all day he is in his laboratory experimenting and calculating. And my mother does not understand him. She thinks he is wasting his life: she would have liked him to go out with her and see crowds of people, and laugh and be merry. But he does not understand this. Sometimes I think he is even contemptuous.

So they live on and their love is a burden to them: for they love each other still. And I might please my mother by being sociable and merry, or my father by taking an interest in his scientific research, but all day I can think of nothing but music. So I too am isolated. Sometimes I wish that I had no love for art, that I might have and give a human love that is not all pain: but it will never be; my mother, my father, and myself will go on living from day to day in the same house, and we shall never come nearer to each other. But one day we shall all recognise that it is impossible and acknowledge it, and perhaps this will be more painful than it was before.

I remember once, when I was a few years younger, arguing with my mother about the view of life that it was natural to take. Of course I was pessimistic. For a time we argued quietly. But, when I refused to allow that life was worth living, my mother grew angry. I think she guessed at my suspicion of her own unhappiness. She rose from her chair and the colour came to her pale face.

'I'm not unhappy' she said, choking down her emotion. 'I have great comforts and I thank God for them. I should have one comfort more if my daughter [and I fancied she winced as she said the word] were less rebellious and more thankful for the life that has been given her,' and she left the room hurriedly and almost in tears.

All the guests are assembled, and I must dress to go down. Which dress shall I wear? I feel as if I should like to put on the old black one, but I cannot be so cruel.

15th March.

I behaved very well yesterday, and actually played the piano to my relations, which was a great surprise to everybody. At first I had a great desire to play the 'Dead March,' but with some difficulty I overcame it and substituted a novelette of Schumann, which was greeted with the usual 'Charming,' 'Delightful,' and so on. I stifled my anger, and went on as if I were

practising to myself. Then I played the
'Carnaval.' When I came to 'Aveu' the room
was absolutely quiet. My relations were evidently impressed with the ability of my performance, for they paid great attention,
although they could hope for little understanding. The room was lighted with lamps
under soft pink shades.

At a small table, on which one of these was
placed, my father sat with his eyes on a book
as if heedless of the music that he heard.
'Aveu' is the most exquisite part of the whole
'Carnaval.' I played it without once looking
at the piano, for I could feel every note perfectly.

When I had played as far as this, my father's
eyes rose from the book and fell on me with
such a look of horror that my fingers almost
froze, and it was with the greatest difficulty

that I managed to play to the end. When I looked at my father again he had resumed his expression of indifference to what was going on. But that melody in 'Aveu' must have aroused some painful reminiscence, for I am positive that it was not my fancy that he looked so frightened. I dare not ask him, but I am determined to find out what is the mystery in his life which makes him shrink so instinctively from music. It must be associated with some one of whom he was very fond; I feel sure of that. But I wish I knew more. I have a suspicion that he has taste, if not passion for music, and that he stifles it in my presence. For what reason?

16th March.

I have been thinking all this morning over what happened last night. I have played the 'Carnaval' up to the point at which my father looked at me so strangely, and I have tried to see some tragedy in the notes, but without success. They are exquisitely beautiful, but it cannot be the music alone that produced the result. I am determined now to find out. I have never seen my father exhibit any emotion but once. Then I came unexpectedly one evening into his study and found him in tears over a letter, and I fancied I saw him hastily slip a photograph into the envelope when I entered. A letter of an old friend who had died, I supposed, and I thought no more about the matter. But the whole scene rose to my mind this morning whilst I was thinking over the occurrence of last night, and trying to account for it. Perhaps his dead friend used to play the 'Carnaval.' But, then, why should he have remained calm until that one passage in the 'Aveu'? And then his look was of horror, not of grief, and so the two scenes have no connection that is obvious.

21st March.

The weather is cold and bleak; the tiny green shoots look nipped. I went out this morning and came back with my eyes aching from the wind, and my hair all over my face.

Nothing new, and my old boredom is beginning again. I am even tired of composing, and have left my work for a time till I feel fresh inspiration. I have worried and worried to get at reasons to account for my father's conduct, but with no result. Till I find some sort of clue I must give up thinking about it.

23rd March.

I can't give up thinking about it. I want to know how his friend died. Perhaps whilst he was playing the 'Carnaval,' but I dare not ask.

How the wind howls! Another note—more like a human voice than anything. I must write a London symphony, with all the noises in London as my material. I will have a fugue-like arrangement of the coster's whistle, and then all the street 'calls,' and romantic interludes of wind and traffic.

My mother talks now of the coming 'season,' and how many dinners we must give, and what invitations we are likely to receive. I expect we shall see the usual number of uninteresting people, who will talk incessantly about the most ridiculous trifles in an important way. Then there will be the crowd of suitors too. Lately I have been free from them, as I plead convalescence, and stay in my room when they call.

My mother and I fell to talking about marriage the other day, and, as usual, I flew off at a tangent whilst she was revolving round a circle of platitudes. We ended the conversation without an open rupture. I was sullen and my mother was grieved.

Why am I not married? My life might be happier if I were the mistress of a family that I loved. Ah, there is the difficulty. I feel no reliance on any of the people whom I have seen as yet, except one; but even that is in all probability a romance built up by my fancy. How can I know what sort of husband he would make, or even if he would like to be my husband? Besides, I have only seen him twice, and shall probably never see him again, except in those phantoms that my brain creates, for what else can they be?

But I can still wait. I am not afraid of losing my beauty. Till now it has been in the ascendant as far as I can judge.

All this about myself. Yet all my beauty and my music do not always satisfy me.

Sometimes I could wish that some saviour would come and tell me that art is only the smallest, the least human part of humanity. I could wish that he would say to me, 'Give up music, look round you at the world, and spend your power upon the helpless.' But the saviour does not come. I see no champion of humanity, by whose victory over me I could feel exalted. They are all so petty and so mean, and I turn aside and find that there is an absolute beauty in music, and when the human voice in me is still my music satisfies me. But when the human voice cries out, I think it tells me that the love of music is a sensual passion, and that I ought to crush it, but I cannot: it is stronger than myself.

There are times when I feel that I would like to end the struggle, but I have not the courage. Besides, I will not be responsible for interfering in my life.

28th March.

The winds are over, at least for the present. April is anticipated by a few days.

Showers, blue sky, and broken white clouds, through which the sun struggles. How amusing it is to see all the people run when the rain begins. Why? Not because they are afraid of spoiling their clothes — no, there must be a deeper reason than that. It seems to me as if, like cats, they had an instinctive repugnance to the feeling of wet. Just as animals run to their holes, they skurry along to some place of shelter.

Out comes the sun again and shines with steady, intense beams. Out they creep again as if they were doing some wrong for which the rain had punished them, and were only just prepared to risk being detected again.

As I watched them I found myself humming a melody of light satire. I can't remember having heard it anywhere before.

Does not this fragment seem to form a comment on the scene—blue and white sky, and the sun struggling through a shower, while the people creep in and out of doorways?

5th April.

Bad weather again, and everything seems to go wrong. I can't compose. I am exhausted, and I feel a numbness over all my faculties.

This afternoon a cousin of mine came in to tea. She is a pretty, innocent girl, and every one is fond of her; but I am bored by her. She tires me with her ceaseless chatter of trifles, and she never seems tired herself. She has a sort of eternal freshness about her that wears me out. Of course I was sullen and depressed. She wore her hair in a new fashion. I asked her what was amiss with her head. But she was quite unconscious of my unkind satire. She put her hand to the back of a silky knob of hair, and lightly turned the conversation.

She is going to be married, and she babbled about the husband she was going to have. I sat back and listened to her description with a blank feeling. She told me of a man tall and fair, with a fair moustache and large blue eyes. She said he was a captain in the army, and she told me how he would come and tell her of his experiences in the battlefield. How I hated the man without seeing him! A great blundering heavy fellow with the Philistine good looks!

But I listened to her prattle, and felt a weariness when I looked at her.

She sat in a low easy-chair. She has such a pretty childish face, and she played with the parasol on her lap as she spoke. As I looked at her, I began to wonder why I too could not laugh and be happy like this. And then I felt angry and irritated by the sight of her.

After she had left they said I behaved very coldly to her, and I fancy I saw a look of jealous pain in my mother's eyes when her engagement was mentioned.

I have come to a new resolution: I will go out again and see if I can work off my nervous excitement. This time I will try and act all sorts of different parts, according to the people whom I meet. This will give me plenty of excitement, if I can keep up my poses successfully. I suppose some people would think it very wrong to act in this way, but I must get through my life somehow, and why should I sacrifice my peace of mind to other people's view of morality?

I think my scruples at offending this morality grow weaker and weaker every day. After all, the deference that I pay to a certain number of conventions is only due to a circumstance. I have no innate sense of right and wrong. But I have a sense of self-preservation. I feel that I cannot go on as I have been for some time. My real personality is an impossible one. It dissatisfies, tires, and frightens me. So I shall create a fictitious one, and there shall be no deity to meddle with the creation of that. Perhaps after all he would not be so anxious to claim this creation for his own. But it shall be terribly exciting. I will use all my powers. If I lose my own identity in one of the poses that I assume, I cannot be worse off than I was before. But there is no likelihood of that. Myself will cling to myself through everything. I can feel that.

8th April.

The last few days have passed more pleasantly. The weather is bright and warm, and I feel in better spirits. I don't want to play the piano much, but I am taking much more interest in the things round me. I have been shopping several times with my mother, and have gone through it very creditably.

Yesterday we had a long discussion over a dress which I am to wear at a garden fête in the evening. I wanted all one colour, but my mother wanted a contrast. We compromised the matter. I am to have a scarlet silk dress, but I shall wear a large black velvet bow, with a diamond spray in my hair. My mother is enraptured with me for taking so much interest in my dress. I am watching it all with strange curiosity. I fulfil my part easily at present. What will happen later I don't know.

13th April.

I spend my time less and less at the piano, and occupy myself with reading and writing. I am watching my new self closely, and shall make a faithful and accurate record of what happens.

My father is frankly pleased at my bestowing less attention on music. He is becoming more communicative. I pretend to have a diminished interest in my favourite pursuit. We talk together about books.

28th April.

Another fortnight past, and I think I have behaved very well. Everybody in the house is pleased with me. I have become very fashionable, and dress three times a day.

In the morning I put on a soft grey dress very loose (the dressmaker calls it *négligé*), and I lounge about for a few hours in easy chairs. Sometimes I hold a French novel in my hands and lazily turn over the pages. The yellow cover is a most useful property.

I caught sight of myself in the looking-glass the other day, just as I had settled into my morning position, and was much amused at the perfectness of the pose. After lunch I dress my hair in the new fashion, and put on an afternoon dress for the Park. My mother and I drive up and down and look at the ceaseless repetition of fashionable faces. Then we come home and have tea, at which there are not unfrequently a crowd of youths who dangle and simper. In the evening we go to a theatre, which I don't like at all, or sometimes to a dinner-party.

30th April.

Yesterday we had had a very tiring day, and I had not had a moment to myself till when I went to my room to go to bed.

I went to the pier-glass. As I stood in front of it I saw a tall, elegant figure, in a pale yellow silk dress, open at the neck, with large sleeves trimmed with cream-coloured lace. On her neck were stones that sparkled and shone. The hair was compactly dressed. In it was a fan-shaped comb all jewelled. The general impression was one of extreme elegance, and there was a touch of coquetry in the pose—the head thrown back slightly on one side; the large dark eyes half closed.

Something in the subtle grace of this figure startled me.

I let down my hair quickly, almost tore my dress off, jumped into bed, and put the light out. So I lay for a long time with my eyes staring at the darkness, thinking and wondering at my transformation. I felt that it was a strain, and that it could not go on, but I could not foresee what was to terminate it. Then I fell asleep through sheer exhaustion.

1st May. 10 *o'clock a.m.*

This is the month of lilac and laburnum—almost my favourite month in the year. How delicious the air is. I am quite looking forward to the garden fête to-night. The green shoots are throbbing with vitality. There is a soft haze in the air, and the sun shines lazily and gently. I can hear the songs of the birds from my window.

2nd May. 2 *a.m.*

What a strange experience to-night has been. Surely now I can have no doubt that any morality I might have is an accident. How it happened I don't know. And what a brute he was, too—the sort of creature that I loathe. But I felt so irresponsible.

I will try and put it all down as it happened.

My father could not come with us; he had to attend some patients with whom he had appointments. The night was glorious, and my mother and I drove in an open carriage, for the air was mild. The streets were crowded. We had to drive through suburbs full of poor people attracted from their houses by the splendour of the evening. Many of them sat bareheaded at their doorsteps, and watched their children playing in the road. What quantities of them there seemed to be, of all ages, and they were playing different sorts of

THE MIRROR OF MUSIC

games on the pavement. Every now and then the white moonlight fell upon a group of them hopping over spaces chalked on the stone flags. Sometimes they would hurrah as the carriage whirled by, and the babies would stretch out their little hands towards us and coo with delight.

My mother prattled about the people we should meet, and what sort of illuminations would be in store for us. I did not pay much attention. My eye had caught the figure of a tall, fair girl at the corner of a little lane, with a child in her arms. She looked after us in a wondering way as we passed.

I was making up to myself a piece of her life on that evening. She was to wander back to a neat little cottage with a tiny garden in front of it, and a border of flowers. Here was to be a man leaning over the gate, with a pipe in his mouth. I could see the smoke curling up into the moonlight. She was to go up to the gate and hold up her child for the admiration of the man. I could see him throw up his head and jerk out the smoke before he caressed the child.

The carriage stopped and prevented my continuing the scene. My mother, in a slightly irritated voice, told me to get out. It must have been about half-past ten. We were ushered into the presence of the hostess by a flunkey. The garden was full of people exquisitely dressed. I soon remembered what was expected of me, and talked glibly about the 'beautiful weather,' 'so fortunate,' 'delightful scene,' and 'not a bit cold.' Then I slipped away from my mother to talk to some people at a little distance from us, whom I had met before.

We stood at the edge of the large lawn in front of the house. It was dotted with people. I did not mind the women, they looked so beautiful; but the men in their black dress coats, with their tall, straight figures, how bizarre they seemed in this framework of nature at her most glorious season.

A little zigzag pathway led through a maze of bushes next to where we stood. I stole softly along it to enjoy the beauties of the night away from the sight of those hideous black figures that marred the scene on the lawn.

It was a short path, and led on to a bowling-green surrounded by a row of bushes backed by tall, waving trees. I walked across the green, which felt like velvet under foot, and stood at the other end, rapt in wonder and delight at the beauty which lay before me.

The moonlight fell on bushes teeming with pale green, it lit up the dew that had fallen, making it dance and sparkle, and the smell of the damp earth throbbing with the fruit of the new season inspired me with a sort of ecstasy.

I sank into an old wicker seat and breathed in the pure soft air. Then an exquisite pain shot over my whole body as this floated into my mind :—

Music had not exerted its power over me so strongly for some time. I murmured Schumann's song until I felt almost as if I were growing into the trees or being melted into the moonbeams.

I was disturbed by hearing a dry crackle on the gravel pathway. Instinctively I pulled at a branch of leaves that swung above me, and appeared as if I were occupied in examining it. The sudden pull had shaken the dew into my face. I looked intently at one of the leaves, and watched a little insect trying to disentangle itself from the fine web of hair with which the leaf was covered. The moonlight was so strong that I could see every movement of the tiny creature.

A man stood before me. I looked up, still clinging to my branch.

'Botanising?' he said in a heavy, awkward way.

He was just the sort of man for whom I have a particularly strong feeling of repugnance: tall, fair, and what would be called good-looking.

He asked if I was not afraid of catching cold. Would I not take a turn round the garden with him? I looked down again at my little beast, who had just got one leg free, and was flourishing it about at a tremendous rate, but his innumerable other legs were still too intricately entangled to be disengaged.

My sentimental mood had passed: it had been dispelled by the appearance of the figure in front of me. I let the branch fly back into its place, while a momentary wonder passed through my mind as to the fate of the insect. Then I rose and took the arm of the man who stood before me, and we walked together.

As I think of it all now, it seems to me as if my real self followed behind us; for, when I try and imagine the scene, I see the scarlet figure of a woman leaning on a tall man's arm and walking on, whilst a sort of horror seizes me at the conduct of the woman, but I can never come close enough to her to stop her. I seem bound to follow at a fixed distance.

I know that I felt as if I should like to play with this man, to act the part of a wicked woman to him, and see how he would receive me. So I talked lightly and toyed with a flower in my dress, and once I stopped and looked at him strangely and then pretended to look confused. I can't think what we talked about, but the next thing I remember is, that his eyes looked at me in a new way, and then he caught hold of me and a sort of horror possessed me; he was so vile, such an animal, and I loathed him, but, by a sort of irresistible fascination, I was compelled to encourage him.

Here again I see my other self walking behind in an intense agony at the behaviour of the woman in scarlet with whom I feel myself to be inseparably connected. I can see it all, and I can feel the despair.

She looked at him with languorous eyes, and he embraced her violently, and then kissed her passionately with his coarse lips. I can feel it now, and his strong breath smelt of the smoke of cigarettes. I could have killed him, but out of the pose that I had taken up, came a part of myself that clung to him. I could not battle with it. It was a new enemy in league with him. They both fought against me, so that I could not even repulse his familiarities.

I was conscious of my impotence, and with a horrible anxiety waited for what was to come next. We heard talking close to us. A thick bed of shrubs was all that separated us from the lawn in front of the house. We had walked aimlessly, and were now only a few yards from the people whose voices we heard. It was like awakening from some terrible nightmare. At last I felt safe, and slipping my arm out of his, I stole quietly on to the lawn.

'How untidy your hair is, my dear,' said my mother.

'The air has blown it about,' I replied calmly, as I quickly arranged it with my hand.

Soon afterwards we went home, and I listened in silence to my mother's comments on the arrangements. I felt stupefied—a hard sodden feeling—and stared at the white moon as the carriage drove home. She had witnessed my shame and still shone steadily upon me, pitilessly, I thought.

So, after all, I have not a grain of morality. There is only a very little that distinguishes me from the people I saw in Piccadilly that night. How long ago it seems!

Just the distinction of circumstance, that is all. And this is the result of my new resolution. What does it matter what I do? The end is always a sense of crushing misery; the world is too much for me. I may flourish about as I please, but I shall not escape from it any more than the little insect from the leaf.

15th May.

Everybody is enraged with me. I have refused to go to several entertainments at the very last moment simply because I felt depressed and melancholy, and knew that a crowd of strangers would make me worse. There is something in the mere presence of other people that affects me instantly. I can feel the difference distinctly when I am playing the piano alone, and when there are others in the room. When I refused to go out I felt that this influence would frighten me more than ever; for there are times when I feel an indescribable terror at the approach of some unknown catastrophe. This is increased when there are others with me. I see them sitting before me and feel that I shall have to face something from which they cannot save me, and the consciousness of their impotence to help me, in case the catastrophe were to happen, makes me dread its approach all the more, and sometimes even imagine that it is come.

I cannot tell this to my mother, she would

not understand, or she would say that I must see a doctor. My father has grown gloomy lately, since I have begun to work hard at the piano again. I have laid aside my beautiful dresses. I don't care to see their brilliant colours, and I have not forgotten the woman in scarlet. So it is all as before, and they are annoyed and angry with me.

In the meanwhile, I am racing ahead with my great work. The rest seems to have done me good, and I can write more quickly and more easily than before. I think of nothing else now. I compose for hours together. I write with the window open; for I love to smell the spring air laden with the scent of the lilac, which is now in full blossom in the square.

27th May.

The meaning of Schumann's *Vogel als Prophet* has just dawned on me. I have played it a hundred times, and until now never knew what it was; and now I can only feel very strongly an intense beauty which I cannot define.

I started by seeing in it merely an exquisite

elegance of construction. This is as far as I reached, after hearing it about fifty times. After I had grasped fully its structural peculiarity, I awoke to a sense of its extraordinary musical beauty, and forgot all about the subtle pattern of the notes. In fact, I then arrived at the essential beauty of the thing.

The preliminary stage required an intellectual grasp, but it was only a medium through which I ultimately passed to the real thing. So much for those who talk about intellectual appreciation. I think I have hit them over this point. My old curiosity in the sources of music is arising again.

June 1st.

I inaugurate the month with a debauch in Chopin.

The sun is hot, and there is blue mist in the distance that promises more heat to come. I don't mind however hot it becomes. The glorious summer is upon us now.

There is such a generous feeling of life about it, life in the streets amongst men who talk and laugh as they feel the hot sun on their backs, and amongst the birds that sing loud and long, hastening from tree to tree to rejoice with their fellows over the warm bright season; and there is summer amongst the insects on the soft earth. How they swarm about. I watch them in my flower-boxes in the windows of my room. People who are dull and dead in the winter come out of their shells and talk kindly and pleasantly. I think we say different things in the winter when we are cramped with the cold and stay indoors as much as possible. Our egoism has a larger field on which to show itself.

But now the glorious yellow sun is shining, and the flowers are leaning forward and stretching up their heads to catch his warm beams. And there are gorgeous colours blended in perfect harmony everywhere, not the artist's harmony, but the harmony we know to be in nature's universal throb. The green leaves are laughing lazily in the boughs as they sway to and fro with a gentle breeze. The dust of the streets has not soiled them yet.

Then there are calm star-lit nights, and the ceaseless shuffle of lovers' feet on the pavement below.

June 8th.

I have spent a whole week at the great Chopin Sonata. What splendid work! It has suggested another question to me.

Is there not a distinction between such music as is derived from the material within the composer and such as is derived from that without?

Roughly speaking, I think it is in this that lies the main difference between Beethoven and Chopin. The latter has a strong personality which pervades nearly all his works, while the former cannot be detected in his compositions any more than Shakespeare in his plays. But in this great sonata there is very much less evidence of 'character' writing than in anything else that Chopin has done.

The difficulty is not at an end here, for sometimes the material inside the composer coincides with external material, and now to come to an illustration which is the crowning point of all this. The following quotation from the sonata contains a sort of double paraphrase, that is, a paraphrase of Chopin's personality united with a paraphrase of a natural phenomenon which I will explain shortly:—

THE MIRROR OF MUSIC

Now so far there is a double paraphrase. It is typical Chopin melody, but it also contains a paraphrase (*not* a translation) of the following physical phenomenon.

The sun is shining lazily on a stream which flows gently on the surface, but has a stronger undercurrent. The water is clear and long reeds stretch upwards to within about a foot of the surface. There is a small deep pool formed by an irregularity on the banks of the stream. Here the reeds wave their heads lazily from side to side. This is the melody in the treble, whilst the bass represents the steady current of the main stream. This blending of paraphrases continues only as far as the passage quoted.

Then comes a piece of pure Chopin paraphrase which has nothing in common with a natural phenomenon :—

This is a piece of purely internal writing, as most of Chopin's writings seem to me to be.

June 13*th.*

My father looks ill and worried. I cannot guess the reason, but I feel that I am mixed up with it in some mysterious way. More than once I have caught him looking at me critically, almost as he would look at one of his patients. He is watching me, I am sure. The other day my mother entered the room with a large bowl of red peonies. I shuddered involuntarily.

Perhaps they reminded me of the scarlet dress. But their colour is different, not so hard and bright, but a dull, rich, heavy red. My father had noticed me and, looking eagerly at me, hastened from the room.

What can it all mean? And they do not talk to me now, but I feel as if they had some secret understanding with each other about me.

Well, what does it matter? I have my music, which shall be everything to me now, for I am growing less and less in touch with the life at home with its eternal repetition of domestic trivialities.

I shall write hard and try and finish my work by the end of this month. Nothing shall stop me. I will listen to no objections. I feel in the vein now and I will write, write, write. I shall have put a large portion of my life into this work of mine, and then, perhaps, no one will perform it.

'Perhaps?' Very likely. But I must write.

June 28*th*.

In the early part of this morning I walked down Oxford Street. The sun shone brilliantly on the shops, and brought out strongly the colours and patterns displayed in their windows. I was in a very musical frame of mind. I saw nothing real in these objects, but they seemed to suggest sounds according to their colour and shape.

One large window was filled with nothing but soft round hats of many different colours. It was only afterwards that I knew that they were hats. At the time, I saw nothing but a mass of rounds of varying shades and they seemed to express sound. There was music everywhere. I could not look at anything without imagining that it was existent only in relation to a musical standard.

In another window there was a definite scheme of brass rods placed one below the other. On these were hung gloves at intervals: one row slanting to the right, one to the left, and so on. Here again, whilst I looked, I could see only the scheme of lines and colours, and they did not convey a pictorial effect to me, but the effect of sound. How mad it seems! but I am music-mad to-day.

The great work is nearly finished. There are two melodies which came into my head this afternoon. I wonder whether the gloves and the hats have anything to do with them?

30th June. 2 *a.m.*

I have finished, and there is a deafening roar in my ears. I can hear every note of it. I am certain that it is a triumph. I can scarcely see anything round me, but all my senses seem to have become absorbed into hearing. I cannot keep quiet. It is so exciting.

It seems to have possessed me. I cannot do anything but listen. The score is on the table, but I do not see it—only I hear the gradations of the orchestra and the voices rising higher and higher.

I thought I saw Severine's head and shoulders on the window-pane suffused with light and the eyes beaming with enthusiasm. . . . Gone.

But listen, listen how the sound surges about. And they are singing magnificently. Higher, higher, it rises. Now I cannot distinguish the instruments and the voices. It is one great sound. I can . . .

Why did everybody rush to my room? They

were all terribly agitated about something. My father looked very pale. He was trembling all over.

'Why did you scream?' he said in a strange voice. 'Tell me, dear, why? What is it? Has something frightened you?' Then he saw the table strewn with sheets of manuscript music and he shook all over.

'It is very wrong of you to wear yourself out like this: why must you sit up to such hours in the morning? Have you not time?'

As far as I can make out from their queer looks and scraps of phrases when they rushed up, they found me standing in a rigid position in the middle of the room, with my eyes wide open as if staring hard at something which they could not see. They had come in answer to a piercing shriek which they had heard from my room.

It must have been when I heard all the instruments and voices blending into one sound rising higher and higher, till I felt that I must sing, and I must have cried out like some mad creature.

1st July.

I am terribly exhausted and have done

nothing all to-day, but sit at the open window with my eyes half closed. They ache terribly, and I feel a lassitude creeping all over my limbs.

How sweet the limes smell! The air is full of perfume. I feel as if I were just recovering from a great illness. Everybody in the house looks scared. I must have alarmed them terribly. I cannot remember what took place in the interval between the writing of the words 'I can—' in my diary and the arrival of the people in my room. But my father perplexes me. Why does he watch me so anxiously? I shall watch him and try and find out.

3rd July.

This watching is terrible. I am sure that there is some tragedy that my father is concealing from me, but what it is I cannot guess. I am determined, now that my work is finished, to find it out. My father is less anxious now that I have deserted the piano again. Quite consistent. I have been looking at 'Aveu' again to see if it will give me any clue.

14th July.

How does the time pass? I don't know, for I have given up playing or composing for a time. I can do nothing but think, and think over my father, and try to imagine what can account for his horror of music.

I became very bold this morning with him. We were sitting out together in the square. For some time we talked about all sorts of trifles, and then the conversation flagged. We both leaned back on the seat, and watched the carriages passing up and down. Every now and then we said, 'How hot it is.' Then quite suddenly I turned round and, looking straight at his face, I said quietly but earnestly,

'Why have you such a horror of music?' I trembled after I had spoken. I almost wished that I had not asked the question: yet I felt, as soon as the words were out, that I had nothing to do with them, and I waited, with the curiosity of a third person, for an answer.

A deep sadness came into my father's eyes, but there was scarcely a trace of the old anxiety.

'Some other time, dear,' he said absently;

'it is a sad story, and I feel too happy now to wish to refer to it.'

Always the same evasion. I knew while I asked him that he would not tell me. But I will find out. I must find out. I feel as if I have a right to know.

20th July.

We are going away soon. There was a good deal of discussion as to what place we should select. Finally, we agreed to go to Dinard. I did not care much what place was chosen, but I shall be glad to get away. I want to forget the last six months entirely, and start afresh. I can only do this by forming new associations in a new place. We are to start in about ten days.

23rd July.

All is preparation. Endless dresses are being bought. My mother has started packing already: there are countless things to be thought of, though what they are, I cannot imagine. I am only in the way whenever I try to do anything, so I leave everybody to be as busy as they please, and I retire to my own room. In this way I also escape seeing the visitors who call and discuss with absorbing interest their plans for travelling.

People are leaving London in crowds. From my window I watch the houses opposite and see the trunks being handed down the stairs into the hall, and the children standing about in the way with an eager excited look on their little faces. How they love this going away.

I remember my own intense joy in travelling when I was a child. How thrilling—the idea of taking a journey, perhaps even on the sea, and then arriving at a foreign country, where they talked differently, and perhaps sleeping in a railway carriage at night (the most exciting of all). I think what I liked best in travelling was that we were all on an equality. I did what my parents did, and what is more, my parents had to act in my childish way. It was as refreshing to think of them having to sleep without a proper bed, and with only half their clothes off, as if they had played at rocking-horse or something.

25th July.

Still more bustle and excitement.

I have been looking at my musical manuscripts and wondering what is to become of them. I have no one to whom I can show them: all my musical friends have been studiously kept away from me for the last few years, so that I have lost sight of them. This must have been my father's doing. Strange, how consistent all his conduct is in this one thing.

28th July.

At last I have found it all out, and I am terribly frightened. Why had I such a thirst to know it? Now it is too late and I cannot escape the knowledge. Why—

But what is the good of all this regretting. I tried to discover it because I was compelled to try and discover it. There is no reason for such things.

The stars are coming out one by one. They blink at me as I write. I must shut the window. They shall not see my misery—besides I don't want the beautiful night. I have nothing to do with it. I think I hate it.

At about six o'clock I peeped into my father's study. The door was ajar and he did not see me, but I saw him put something at which he had been looking into a small drawer in his writing desk. Instantly I remembered the photograph over which he had cried that day when I had discovered him. My curiosity was aroused. I stole away unnoticed.

A few minutes afterwards, a servant brought a note summoning my father to attend a patient at once. He immediately left the house. When he was gone I crept into his study and went to the drawer into which I had seen him put the thing he had been examining. I did not pause for a moment, but drew it out swiftly. In it lay a book covered in green plush: very old and worn, with a small gold clasp to it. I took it out to see if there was a photograph underneath, but there was nothing else in the drawer. Then I softly unfastened the clasp. The book gaped in one part, evidently from the insertion between the leaves. It fell open at this part. The pages were covered with a very fine manuscript writing, the ink of which had faded into a faint brown, and the paper had become yellowish. Between the leaves lay a small oval daguerreotype. It was the picture of a woman. The face was very lovely and the eyes were magnificent, but they were without expression. In the hair,

THE MIRROR OF MUSIC 97

which was very thick, was wound a scarf.
Something fascinated me in the face. I looked
at it for a long time. Then I looked again at
the manuscript. I took it to the window. It
was written in Russian; but I could trace
characteristics of my father's handwriting in it.
It was a diary, and the page at which I opened
it was dated thirty years ago.

With some difficulty I read the two pages at
which the book had fallen open. They were
written whilst my father studied at the University in St. Petersburg in '50, and contained
an account of a drinking bout with fellow-students. It had been followed by a dance at
some tavern; there was just enough in the
words to make it certain that the whole thing
was not very reputable.

But what had this to do with the daguerreotype? The face was that of a woman of about
forty years of age. I concluded that the
picture must have been slipped into this place
fortuitously. So I turned over the leaves and
read a little further. There was more description of student life. Occasionally an allusion to a concert in very enthusiastic terms,
frequent allusions to letters from home.

G

About a year later than the date at which I had opened the book, there was a poem on a nocturne of Chopin dedicated to the writer's mother, Elizabeth Kaftal. Then it struck me that the daguerreotype must be of her, and I looked once more at it, and gained fresh conviction from the likeness in certain features, which I traced between the picture and my father.

A little later was an entry stating that his mother looked ill and tired, and there was a comment to the effect that she exhausted herself too much in her profession. 'She can never leave her music, and we all love it so much that we do not help to keep her from it.' Then they went into the country for the mother's health and there the tragedy happened. Why did I ever read it?

In the country she grew worse. At times she was delirious and did not know those round her. Then she would sing about the house in a strange way that frightened people. One night the sleeping household was aroused. They heard the shuffling of feet below. They took lights and went down. The drawing-room door was open and there was a swift current of air. They hurried in—the candles flickered with the draught, and there they saw her at the piano.

She had crept down in her night-dress, and opened the French windows facing the lawn, to let in the cool air. The moonlight poured into the room. She sat at the piano playing exquisitely, whilst her eyes stared in a dull senseless way. When she saw them she began to sing, and her voice was soft and low. She sang the melody of 'Aveu' whilst she played with her delicate sensitive touch. Suddenly she burst into loud hysterical laughter, and then fainted away. They carried her upstairs. She had lost her reason and never recovered. For a few years she lived with a guardian in a house in St. Petersburg. One morning they found her dead in her bed, and on the floor was a crumpled bit of paper with the first few notes of 'Aveu,' written in pencil.

Now I have told it all. It is so clear, so easy to understand. My father's fears and . . .

Perhaps I am mad already. Certainly, many people would call me mad, but I am not, no— I know that I am not. Am I not conscious of everything that I do? much too conscious.

Perhaps that is a sort of madness. Perhaps they have been treating me as mad all along and I have not noticed it. I have been tricked. But they shall see that I know their secret thoughts. Oh! to get away from it all. I dare not think. How late it must be. I will go to bed.

29th July.

No rest all night. I was haunted by the thing that I had read. I can see the figure at the piano in the moonlight. She is so beautiful. Ah! the pitilessness of it.

I am not sure of myself. Every movement I make I think to myself: is it sane? Do you know what you are doing? I look at myself in the looking-glass. I, too, am beautiful, very beautiful. I think I never was so beautiful before.

After all, what do I care? I shall not trouble myself. I shall allow myself to drift on without a struggle. I am not responsible. They say there is a God.

30th July.

They are packing, packing, packing. There is a look of triumph in my mother's eyes. I suppose she has been wrestling with a hat-box or something, and has finally vanquished it, and it has sunk sullenly into its place in the trunk.

They noticed this morning that I looked very pale. I said I had not slept, and this comforted them. Many people when they are ill worry themselves and other people incessantly until they can fix on a cause to which to attribute their malady. When they have settled this they seem to be satisfied. But, though I know too well the cause of my fear, it does not satisfy me. It makes me tremble.

How hot it is! I think I shall steal out for a walk in the streets. It is only nine o'clock; perhaps I can forget myself there in the contemplation of other people.

I feel stupefied and dazed.

As I walked along through the gas-lit streets, in a large plate-glass window I caught sight of the reflection of the shop opposite with the row of gas-lamps over its front. These looked like masses of glimmering gold in the reflection, and they seemed to form a perspective. I walked across the road and gazed at the window. I could see the reflections of the people who were walking along. They looked like dark shadows flitting past. Then I forgot all that was round me, and imagined that the reflection was the reality, and that the real objects lay behind the window, but I was outside them and could not get at them.

I stood motionless staring hard at the window. More shadows flitted past from time to time. 'What a strange world it is,' I thought; then I noticed that there was one figure in the picture that did not move. It stood close to me, but when I tried to look straight at it, it seemed to shrink back and become blurred and indistinct. Suddenly I recognised the motionless figure to be myself. It was a horrible sensation. But it broke my trance, and the noise of the traffic seemed to fall on my ears with redoubled reality. Then I rushed home. Now I am waiting for sleep. I feel as if half the vitality had gone out of me; but something seems to hold up my eyelids though I want to shut them.

JERSEY, 2*nd August.*

I am not tired. It is splendid to be on the sea. How the water tumbled about. It seemed as if we rode on the colossal head of some monster who, every now and then, tossed about his long locks, jerking the boat this way and that. Sometimes we seemed to stand still, sometimes I felt that we were moving, but could not tell in what direction. I stayed on deck the whole time.

The dawn was magnificent. At first the dull, cold look of the sky, and the water looking almost solid, then the growing glory of the sun with a million gradations of colour, until at last there was a blaze of light, and the water flashed and gurgled.

DINARD, *4th August.*

I think I shall love this place. You can see such pretty things from it. In itself it is too overbuilt with villas. But inland and along the coast it is lovely. There are parts where sloping stretches of green come right down to the edge of the little bay, and bright flowers bend over until their heads almost touch the surface of the water. Sometimes the capricious tide leaves broad stretches of bright yellow sand and masses of red gold seaweed, sometimes it fills up every nook on the coast, and licks the rocky side on which the villas are built.

On the opposite side of the bay—St. Malo, with its exquisite maze of elegant spires, which emerge at sunset from a liquid golden mist. And the tiny islets in the middle of the bay, one of them all but covered with a small tower —an atmosphere of diminutive romance hangs about them, especially when they are capped by rose-coloured clouds.

7th August.

I have made up my mind not to think of the past. It has no meaning to me. . As soon as a thing has happened it ceases to have any reality. Sometimes even while it is happening I cannot be certain of its reality. Why should I trouble, then, about the story that I discovered in my father's manuscript? It happened many years ago, and it is already many days since I read it. And yet, the figure of that woman haunts me. I can see her as she sat at the piano in her white night-dress with the moonlight upon her. I can feel the cool air rushing through the windows. How the great eyes stared as she played the exquisite melody of 'Aveu.' She had wandered into another world, and she never found her way out of it.

THE MIRROR OF MUSIC

I am tired of thinking, I will go out.

A delicious afternoon. I wandered along the green border of the bay till I came to an open orchard. I picked out an apple-tree laden with fruit, and flung myself down beneath its shade. The sun was intensely hot, and poured down upon my face through an opening in the branches. Fallen fruit lay everywhere amongst the long grass. The tide had gone far back, leaving strips of grey and gold sand, beyond which the water sparkled and danced in the sunlight.

I closed my eyelids. The sun beat upon them, warm and generous. In the air was a stillness broken only by the buzzing of insects and the sound of a stream at a little distance from where I lay.

Half opening my eyes I saw flashes of white linen and a group of women by the stream, some kneeling, some standing. Then I became dimly conscious of the melody of 'Ich hörte ein Bächlein rauschen'; my eyes closed, and I must have lain there for nearly two hours. Once or twice I gazed straight up at the sun, which darted fiercely upon my eyes, making me shut them instantly, and see white spots floating in a brick-red sea for several minutes afterwards.

11th August.

There are times when I feel bored here—a sort of dull, heavy feeling. When I suffer from one of these attacks I never can conceive anything beyond that on which my eye rests for the moment. I am entirely absorbed by one idea.

This morning I sat and watched the sea, and I could think of nothing but the sea. I could not get away from the idea. Then I turned my back to the sea and looked at the villas, and then I was at once absorbed by them, and so on with every object on which my eyes rested. I could not conceive it in relation to the other objects which surrounded it, until, overcome by a sort of nervous exhaustion, I closed my eyes and thought of nothing. Only I felt a dull, aching discomfort.

12th August.

I am growing restless and discontented again. My work is finished, but I don't know how to get it produced. Who will listen to all my theories on music? Will not everybody either laugh at me for being mad, or shake their fists at me for being unconventional? There is only one person on whom I can rely, and I don't know where he is, or what has become of him since he fought his duel about that girl.

I wonder what has become of him. Perhaps he would not take any interest in me now. He did then. I felt that we attracted each other. I want him now. I want some one to share in my triumph: for my work is a triumph whatever they may say. He would understand it all. Why should I always be isolated in my life. I want to be with some one who understands me, I want to complete myself; and this cannot be whilst I am alone in every thought, in every feeling. I think I would attract him too. I am just as beautiful as I was, far more beautiful than when I saw Severine. My skin is just as white, my eyes are just as large—almost as large as the eyes in the daguerreotype. Besides, I would make him like me. I would exert my power to the utmost. But I shall probably never see him again. If he were near and they knew that I liked him, they would put mountains between us, because of the girl with the *liebes-kranken Augen*, and yet I think I almost envy her in her misery.

13th August.

All last night I was awake. My mind was a blank: I could think of nothing, but tossed about from side to side. It was so hot that I had opened the window and drawn aside the curtains, but not a breath of air came in. Outside all was perfectly still. So I lay—helpless, my eyes wide open, staring at the darkness. They felt so hard and dry. Sometimes, in an agony of unrest, I plunged my head into the pillow. No amount of opiates could have cured me last night; and then there came to me the settled feeling of despair. So I lay motionless waiting for the dawn.

The physical fatigue must have ultimately conquered me. I was just sinking into a disturbed sleep when a chorus of sounds burst on my ears and woke me up to the real things in the world. I tried to keep out the sound. It grew louder. I opened my eyes.

The sun streamed into my room. A crowd of birds had collected on a tree outside my window, and chirped and chattered, growing noisier every minute, and shaking their wings in the fresh morning air.

Oh, the sense of crushing weariness that fell on me. Life was beginning again: the world was waking to the call of nature. Pure, throbbing vitality sounded in the voices of the birds as they poured from their throats.

I was exhausted. I wanted to forget this eternal vitality with which I cannot keep pace, to forget everything in the world. A feeling of physical repulsion came over me as the chatter of the birds grew louder, and they screamed and fluttered about. Dragging myself out of bed, I tottered to the window, which I shut, and then, after pulling together the curtains to keep the light out, crept into bed again and fell asleep.

14th August.

Still unhappy, discontented, vexed, bored. I can't write or read or walk or do anything.

16th August.

The glory of last night has cured me of my melancholy. I feel an almost divine content.

That I should be granted such a revelation! That I, who have been a miserable groaning creature ever since I can remember, should be allowed a happiness so supreme!

How gently the air plays about me as I sit by the open window . . . and the beautiful sparkling sea! To-day I am allowed to look on it in all its beauty, undisfigured by a morbid frame of mind, . . . and the trees with their pale green leaves, through which the sun is shining, . . . and the great laughing sun himself! How splendid nature seems. The very blades of grass seem to throb with joy, joy, joy. The birds sing. There is laughter in their song, the pure laughter of unreasoning happiness.

I have done with pain, regrets, wishes, hopes, I am absorbed in the joy of living.

It is a perfect world to-day. The sun paints it on every glowing thing, the birds sing it, the sea whispers it. And I, too, am a part in this magnificent creation. Who could find fault with it? He is a madman, lock him up. He knows not the world as it is, but only through his disordered fancy.

I must describe how the change came over me. It was like a miracle.

THE MIRROR OF MUSIC 111

This Villa Cristal is a wonderful place with its fairy terraces and grotto-like setting, but I never really appreciated it until last night.

It stands on open ground close to the sea, which it faces on one side. It was a beautiful night and the water was very calm; on its surface was reflected a long, broad shaft of many coloured lights thrown from an illuminated club building which stands further round the bay. I could hear the gentle plash of the water as if it were at my feet; it died away in a ripple, then broke again. There was something strangely luminous about the air. The sky was a deep blue and the stars looked like lamps suspended in it at different lengths—brilliant and calm. It was about nine o'clock. I could dimly see the outline of the tower which rises from a smaller terrace above that on which I was sitting, and which itself is fringed with miniature terraces jutting out, one below the other.

From where I sat, I could see the rocky staircase with its coronet of gas-lamps, and watch the people of Dinard streaming in from the road and taking their seats at little tables to drink coffee and 'bock' and iced syrups in the open air. Under a colonnade, the roof of which is formed by the floor of the terrace above, a band of Tziganes play Hungarian melodies and Strauss valses. Exquisitely perfect was this music led by a fellow in a light blue uniform, who tumbled about as he played his violin like a great dolphin swaying his body to and fro to a marvellous rhythm. Soon the whole place was full and alive with conversation and the bustle of waiters.

A light breeze sent a quiver through the stems of nasturtium that climb at intervals up an elegant fence mounted on a rocky border running round the terrace. The green leaves have a weird look as they flutter in the gaslight.

Yes, it was a wonderful night. The greatness of nature was everywhere: in the cool clearness of the stars, in the plash of the sea, in the softness of the air.

No feeling of awe held me, but I was caressed into a light wonder. There was nothing inharmonious in the chatter of the people nor in the voluptuous grace of the music, which I seemed to enjoy in a sort of transcendental way. It was no longer a mere physical strain on the senses as I had always imagined it before, but there was a universality about it: it seemed no individual arrangement of notes, but an embodiment of music itself. Perhaps this impression was produced by the absolute spontaneity of the execution, perhaps by the singular harmony between the sensation caused by the breeze and the plash of the sea, and that caused by the emotion which the music expressed.

It was an animated scene. Waiters were flying about charged with innumerable trays heavily loaded, people were talking and laughing, there was an occasional click of billiard balls from within, the band was playing vigorously; and yet all this noise and bustle seemed a mere insignificant accident in the wide serenity of the night which was above and all round us: I half closed my eyes and drank in the fresh cool air with a feeling of deep pleasure.

Outside the terrace, seated at intervals on huge mounds of loose light brown earth, were scattered groups of workmen from the neighbourhood dressed in their blouses. There were women too. They sat quite motionless listening to the music and gazing at the terrace stretched out below them. Strangely unreal they looked as they sat there. Every now and then stones and loose earth slipped down the mounds with a faint rattling sound.

A loud clapping of hands at the conclusion of some Hungarian melodies awoke me from my reverie. As the noise abated I opened my eyes. At first I saw nothing distinctly. Gradually I noticed seated on a mound some distance off, separated from the terrace by a tall light netting of wire fringed at the bottom with crockery and creeping nasturtium, a pair of figures.

On the right, a thin-faced man with a scanty black beard, through which shone a sallow complexion. He wore a blue blouse, and his head was covered with a soft black felt hat with the brim turned down. He sat motionless, staring hard with his eager black eyes. Next him on the left, a woman, her head uncovered, with a fine web of tangled black hair loosely straggling from her forehead, a clear pale face, and large dark eyes; the features ordinary. She was dressed simply in a plain dark material. In her arms lay a small child asleep.

My attention was riveted on these figures till I gradually forgot the people on the terrace. There was something so poetical, so mysterious about them; for they did not move, but gazed earnestly at the terrace with their wondering eyes. I began to think they must be creations of my fancy. Then I noticed that the woman's face was serene, godlike in the contentment of its expression. As the music had seemed to me an embodiment of all music—so gradually—I began to see in this woman an embodiment of all womanhood.

. . . .

The child moved slightly. A tiny hand crept round the mother's breast. Over her face spread a divine radiance: the eyes shone. She did not move, but the tiny hand crept up to her cheek and stroked it.

Then I knew why the 'Madonna' was the favourite subject of so many great painters, but the face of this woman was more beautiful than that of any Madonna yet painted. It shone with a strange light as if the moon were upon it, and the fine tangled hair was like an aureole round her head. The head of the child was thrown back now, and the tiny hand was stretching towards the stars and grasping at them.

. . . .

I rose and came within a yard of the mound

on which the figures were seated. There was the network between us. I felt as if it were put there to prevent my going nearer. So I passed up the rocky steps and out, not daring to look behind me for fear that she might be gone.

19th August.

It is all past. I suppose I ought not to grumble. I have had one week's pure happiness. Could I expect it to last longer? For seven whole days I have lived and laughed and loved everything that I could hear or see or feel. I have had no fear, no hatred, no boredom. I have witnessed the glory of the world in its entirety. Little children have smiled at me as I passed. Sometimes I have laughed aloud at the beauty of life. Nothing has seemed incongruous or inappropriate. Everything has happened as it should, as it must happen. I did not want to write or read, for I was filled with a wondering happiness.

But it has all gone. I have sought it in the brightness of the sun, but it is vain glitter to me now. I look for it in the petals of the flower, but it is not there. The sea has become to me

THE MIRROR OF MUSIC 117

like a vast desert, and at night the stars look coldly on me.

I would give all I have for one hour more of that happiness, but the old weary pain has come back to me.

A bee is humming lazily over a flower that creeps in at my window. How the hot sun pours upon him! Nature is playing upon her instrument and the sound is like magic. But I am dumb. My voice will not come to me. My eyes ache with the heat, and my head whirls round.

21st August.

This place has grown hateful to me. I want to leave it. Even the Villa Cristal has lost all its beauty. There is a ghostly feeling about it now. I can only think of my work, and despair of getting it published or produced anywhere.

22nd August.

I have seen him! I have seen him! My brain is on fire. How magnificent he looked, just as when he was playing the Kreutzer Sonata on that wonderful night—so long ago. Severine, Severine, the air seems to ring with it. A thousand faces crowd round me as I write. They are all the face of Severine.

I was standing at the bottom of a little steep road close to the sea, lined with an avenue of trees. There was a breeze that blew up a cloud of dust. The sun was shining fiercely and gilded each grain so that, when he appeared on the brow of the little hill, he was wrapped in a cloud of golden vapour. He stood still for a moment and then, taking his hat from his head, shook himself and breathed in the pure air as he looked down at the little bay below him.

He stood in a 'Velasquez' pose pressing the ground with his feet almost as if he would press it away from beneath him. How splendid he looked with his head thrown back and the black hair in strong relief against the almost deathly whiteness of his skin. I gazed at him until my eyes ached, and I fancied I saw a shadow of a head and shoulders above him, slightly magnified and shivering with an iridescent light caught from the sun. The eyes looked upwards following the point of the bow which I seemed to see drawn right across the violin, as if he had just reached the last note in the passage:

I was leaning against a tree at the bottom of the little road. I did not hear his footsteps. He almost passed me by; then, turning his face on me suddenly, recognised me and came towards me. I was strangely excited. My breath came so hard that I spoke with difficulty.

He was very easy in his manners, bade me walk a little way with him, and asked after my father and mother. This reminded me of the last that I had heard of him, and I thought of the girl who had been ruined by him, but it only flashed across me. Soon we were talking pleasantly together, about all sorts of things. I did not feel as if I had not seen him for so long, and he assumed towards me an attitude which made it possible for me to talk to him with an almost familiar ease. We talked in French. For nearly twenty minutes we walked on, during which I spoke of my work, and he told me that he would look at it, if I would show it him. I was filled with excitement, I knew that he was Director of some Russian theatres, perhaps he could do something for me, and I eagerly promised to show him the manuscript. We parted without making an appointment. He said he would be sure to see me soon, and, with a polite bow, he vanished.

I felt dazed and perplexed. It had all happened so quickly, and till now I had not had time to grasp what it meant. Then I felt vexed that we had not arranged a time to meet again.

How foolish it was! For now how can I tell when I shall see him? I dare not mention to my father or mother that we have met, for they would very likely leave Dinard at once; I don't know where he lives, and perhaps he won't take the trouble to find me out—and yet, I think he will. I fancy that he is interested in me. I must wait until something happens, and yet I feel so restless. Why . . . .

Meanwhile I have something to think about.

August 23rd.

A whole day, and I have not seen him. How weary I am, and yet a sort of faith seems to possess me. He will come again, I know it.

The sea murmurs his name, the wind whispers it. I see him everywhere, in every leaf, in the brightness of the sun, in the cool serenity of the water. Nature seems to be a frame in which to put his glorious picture. Severine, Severine, Severine. . . .

August 24th.

I have seen him again—just for a moment. He asked me when I could come and see him for a few hours to talk over my work. I could not think of any other time than to-morrow evening, when I know my father and mother are dining out with some friends. He slipped a card into my hand with his address on it, and I promised to come then. And now I am waiting for the time to come.

I can do nothing but think of him and all that I knew about him. I see him as he was that night in Moscow so many years ago, and then I try to imagine his conduct in the wicked affair about which I heard. Poor girl! Where is she now. I think I can see a pair of sorrow-stricken eyes that gaze helplessly at me. Is it not a warning to me? Why did I say I would go to him? And yet I must, and besides there can be no harm. I will only stay a little while.

August 25th.

I am dressed and ready. I feel as if I were in a dream. Something has induced me to dress as beautifully as I can. I have put on the dress which I wore at the Lorrimers' dance, and I have twisted a gauze veil over my shoulders and neck. I was dazzled at my own beauty as I looked in the glass just now. To-night I shall not be wasted. Severine will appreciate it. I have had admiration from crowds of men that I hated, now I will have it from one whom I. . .

It is time for me to go.

August 27th.

Out in the open sea with the sails bulging, and the boat lurching over on her side as she spins along. How strange to be here.

The blue water gurgles and hisses as we cut through it, and the sun is pouring down upon us, but there is a fresh breeze that blows my hair about and cools my eyelids.

There are only two others besides myself, a boatman and Severine. They are talking and reefing in the sails now as I write. How the rope grates. In the distance I can see the coast along which we are cruising. Where to? What does it matter? I am still in a dream from which I do not want to wake.

What a beautiful night it was when I went to see him; just such a night as that when I was at the Villa Cristal. He lived in a villa facing the sea, perched high on a cliff a little way out of Dinard. I could hear the sound of his violin floating through the open windows as I neared the house. It was a hot night, and there was not a breath of air from the bay which shone like a silver lake with the light of the moon and stars upon it. The little islets looked like figures emerging from the water, black and mysterious, except where the moonlight caught them, cutting off from the rest the parts which it illuminated. The water was so calm that it scarcely broke at all on the beach. There was only a very faint ripple, and a thin line of silver curled about the yellow beach like the hair about a child's forehead lightly stirred by a breeze.

In front of the house was a tiny wood. The trees seemed to have stretched themselves out as far as they could towards the sky.

When I entered the room I was surprised to see two people besides Severine: an old lady with pretty white hair, and her daughter, a fair tall girl. She had had a music lesson, and the two had been persuaded to stay to supper. I noticed that they were surprised and even shocked at my appearance. Of course I was dressed in a manner to attract their attention, but once I saw the old lady, who wore a lace scarf in her hair, look queerly and fixedly at Severine.

They left soon after I came, and we were alone. I felt nervous and excited at the step I had taken. It was evident that the people who had gone did not look on me very favourably, but I felt no doubt as to staying. How he fascinated me with his great dark eyes that looked so steadily at me. I could not have gone away now if I had been certain of approaching danger.

It was a well-furnished villa, and the room in which he received me faced the bay. I went to the open window and tried to look out. I felt that he was everywhere in the room, and wanted to escape the scrutiny of his eyes.

Then he spoke and asked me if I had brought my manuscript, and seating myself at the window I pointed, without looking round, in the direction of a table on which I had laid it on entering the room. He opened the parcel. I could hear the crackling of the paper, and then he sat still for nearly an hour, and I knew that he was reading it.

How soft the air was ; the sea sparkled, and I felt my hair sweeping across my eyes with a light breeze that had sprung up.

The paper crackled again. I heard a footstep and he stood beside me.

'As far as I have read, it is extraordinary,' he said quietly.

I could not understand what he said. My brain seemed to have gone from me. I was staring hard at the sparkling bay. I repeated the word 'extraordinary' to myself several times before I remembered what it meant. Then I seemed to recover myself, I turned round. He took a seat close to the window and asked me questions about the work that I had shown him. He understood all my fads about words and scenery and seemed struck with wonder that I should have them. Then he asked me to play something to him, but added—

'No, why not play something with me?—— the Kreutzer?'

I shuddered. Something frightened me in his suggestion. But the opportunity was too good to be lost.

'Willingly,' I said, and we went to the piano.

'Do you want music?'

'No. . . . I know it perfectly.'

'And so do I. . . . As it is a fad of yours, let us play in the dark.'

He blew out the candles that stood on the piano. The moonlight came in and fell just where he stood, making his white skin look still whiter.

Oh, how mad I felt as we played! During the first movement I quite forgot where we were. It was as if I were one of two great forces working in absolute sympathy, but working all the time, each straining every nerve to complete the other's part, till the result was a perfect unity in which all individuality was merged. I could neither think nor see. I only felt that I was acting in accordance with some universal law in nature and that nothing could stop me.

With intervals of a few minutes between the movements we played through without a single hitch. When it was over I must have fallen forward, for the next thing that I can remember is the feeling of my knuckles on my eyelids. Then I fancied that the room was filled with a blinding light. Gradually I became conscious that another person was with me, and, as I did so, a horrible feeling of sick repulsion came over me. And finally I came to my senses.

Severine lay staring at me in a low chair near the piano. His bow had fallen from one hand, and the other still clung to his violin which rested its base upon the floor.

. . . .

That night I dreamed again that I was a lily in the midst of a wood, and that I could feel the breath of the wind against my face but could not see; and then I heard steps, and something sharp was cut into the stem, and I was borne away nodding dreamily.

Oh, mother, mother, . . . I have gone from you! You have never understood me, and now the woman in her white dress has claimed me. She is following me about. Just now I fancied I saw her walk across the water towards our boat. . . .

August 28th.

How the train flies along, and how quickly the pictures in the windows change! Beautiful! And it seems as if it were all made for us.

What an exquisite scene just now! A man and woman standing together in a scarlet poppy field upon which the sun streamed. Gone in a flash. Now a packet of little white houses with small yards full of poultry. Now flat open country shut off from us only by a low hedge.

'Hi-i-i—,' shrieks a little fellow, who has clambered up the hedge, and throws up his arms at us as we rush past.

How the telegraph wires dance! They always seem to me to be a symbol of frustrated ambition. They are continually attempting to rise when a pole intervenes and drags them down. Away! Away!! Why should I stop to think? I feel as I do when I am playing the first movement of the *Appassionata*, but more complete. I think Severine is acting the bass for me. Yes, and I am the treble. . . .

Still I think of the *Appassionata*. The sun is down now, and we are at the *Andante*.

August 29*th*.

The country is getting still flatter and poorer. Miles and miles of dull grey fields with a tiny house or a ditch at intervals. An air of desolation over the whole.

Soon we must arrive at our destination.

Moscow, 31*st August*.

Severine has been talking to me about my work, which, he says, he will produce here at the theatre. I am in a whirl of excitement. He is so good to me. I asked him yesterday how he came to know my father, and then he told me that his father and mine were students together in 1845 at the University in St. Petersburg. But in '46 Severine's father married, and went to live at Moscow. When my grandmother died in '53, my grandfather and my father left St. Petersburg, and joined the Maidanoffs.

I asked Severine if he knew anything about Elizabeth Kaftal; he told me that his brother could just remember having seen her when he was taken by his father on a visit to St. Petersburg. He could not have been more than four years old. He heard her play, and when, as children, the two brothers quarrelled, he would laugh scornfully at Severine for not having been born in time to see 'the beautiful lady.' He always talked of her by that name.

September 9th.

How quickly the time flies here! I can scarcely imagine that it is a week or more since I first came. We have been out almost every night. Severine knows so many people, and he says I must be introduced to them, so that they cannot abuse my work when it comes out. He has already given the manuscript to the Opera Company, with instructions to begin as soon as possible. I am to preside at the rehearsals and give my directions. Everything is to be done as I wish. The audience will be in absolute darkness. The orchestra and singing are to be on the stage hidden from view by a thin opaque curtain which will not stop the passage of the sound.

If all goes well, the first performance is to be about the middle of December.

September 15th.

I have not time to think of the past. Everything now depends on the success of my work. Severine is going to play in it. All day long he and I practise together, and in the evening there is nearly always a rehearsal.

To-night a young poet is going with us to hear how we are progressing. I shall dress myself particularly well. Severine likes it, besides I always feel more energetic when I dress in the evening. My old taste for black is quite vanished.

September 30th.

How far away my former life seems already: like a dream. I fancy I can see the old house with its dull grey front. The square is waving with dust-covered branches, and there is a long array of newspapered windows opposite.

People are not back yet from their holiday, but perhaps my mother and father are home again. I wonder what they did when they could not find me. Very likely they are sitting upstairs in the drawing-room looking helplessly at the piano, my only treasure in the great ugly cold room. There is a look of settled gloom on my father's face, and my mother's—.

But what am I doing but thinking of the past? I don't want to think of them. Was it not their fault just as much as mine?

I feel as if I had crept into the frame of the picture of myself which hangs above the piano in the drawing-room at home. It was painted when I was six years old, and on the pale wondering face the artist has put a smile which it never wore. I can feel myself now smiling down upon them as they sit silently in the room opposite each other. I cannot change the smile the painter put. I cannot speak: for it is only a picture, but I long to cry out 'Pity, pity,' . . . and the face smiles on.

I have nearly torn out the page on which I wrote this last entry. What have I to do with regrets? Am I not happy at last? I think I am. It is my own fault if I spoil my happiness by thinking.

My eyes look red, but it will not show by the gaslight. I must hurry off to dress or I shall be late for the rehearsal.

October 3rd.

I have slept badly, and look ill this morning. I fancy I am growing less beautiful. There are lines in my face that were not there before.

These friends of Severine's frighten me. They say such strange things, and I laugh at them, though they make me turn cold. Yesterday they were so boisterous.

I dreamed again of the lily and woke in a deadly terror. I felt as if I were shrivelling up. And then, in the night when all was dark, I fancied I felt a cold, dry finger on my forehead. I could see nothing, but I became certain that the woman in the daguerreotype stood by me. I listened to hear her speak, but she said nothing, and in a minute she was gone, and all I heard was the light rustle of a dress in the wind.

Severine has just been to see me. He was

out all night at a friend's. He was full of what they had done. There was a small party of about eight who met after the rehearsal, and they drank champagne and smoked, and the poet who was with them declaimed a poem called 'Illusion.' It was about a woman's love for a man with the brutality of an animal. Severine said it was magnificent. Then they sang together, and he ended by telling me that most of the others were very drunk before he left. I scarcely answered him, and then he noticed that I was not well, said I must not tire myself so much, and told me to rest for a few days before going to the rehearsals again.

For the first time his company has given me no pleasure. I feel as frightened and depressed as before he came.

October 10th.

The fear has never left me. It never will. Now I know it for certain. It is growing on me. Soon it will overtake me, and then— who knows? My face is growing thinner. Severine himself noticed it, and I can see something else too. My eyes are losing their expression. They seem to grow larger, and all the intelligence is fading from them. I dare not look at myself any more.

This morning I found myself thinking of the mist at the sea when I watched the sunset after my illness. This mist is creeping over me now. I cannot fly from it. Nothing would save me. It will grow, and grow, and grow, until all is darkness, . . . but I will struggle on.

In the meanwhile I have plenty to do. My work is going well. Every one says it will be a triumph. How the melodies sing in my ears. I can think of nothing else. Only another two months, and then the day in my life.

Severine is very kind to me. I cannot tell him what is the matter, but he does all that he can. He seems very distressed that I am changing so much. He wants me to see a doctor, but this I absolutely refused to allow. He grew very angry. In any other frame of mind I should have feared him; as it was, I remained calm and firm. Then he burst out of the room, threatening me with the consequences of my obstinacy, and I did not answer.

October 20th.

Yesterday, as I sat in my room facing the street, I felt as if I were in a dream. Severine was on the balcony, and he addressed a question to me several times before I heard him speak. Then his voice seemed faint and unreal, and as I looked round, all the things in the room wore that soft, unobtrusive look that is peculiar to dreams.

After all, what is our life but a dream? Why should I fear so much? My dream will change: that is all. Perhaps it will be happier.

November 1st.

The leaves are fallen from the trees. This is the season of decay. It suits my mood well enough, but the naked branches look weird by night: like numbers of long thin arms with shrivelled bony fingers pointing—now up to the sky, now down to the earth. What do they mean?

How well the music goes! They sing magnificently, and the orchestra are splendid. All the performers look on me as a deified genius. There is a regular worship at the altar of my work.

The young poet comes very often to the rehearsals with us; once he looked strangely at me, and said, 'Madame est pâle ce soir,' but I took no notice of him. I wonder whether he guesses my secret? Perhaps everybody knows, and they are fooling me. Horrible. I will watch them closely as I used to watch my father.

The struggle is killing me, but it cannot be for long.

November 8*th.*

I am getting weary. It is hunting me down. The thing that I have never been able to define, but that I have felt so unmistakably almost as long as I can remember, is gaining ground.

I have watched the people round me, but they suspect nothing; I must act my part well when they are present, though at times I feel as if I should have to give it up and confess everything to somebody. But to whom?

November 13*th.*

He was right. I am growing pale and thin too. I fancy that people look at me in the streets when I pass by, as if I had some strange deformity.

November 17th.

How shadows terrify me. Yesterday, just as I crept into bed, I saw one on the wall—a huge oval face with waves on each side of it. Then I blew out the candle and tried to forget the shape, but I could not, and lay awake nearly all night.

November 26th.

I am positive that I put my fan last night on a toilet table that stands by the window in my room. We cannot find it anywhere this morning. Who has taken it? No one knows anything about it, but I am certain that it was there last night. Certain? Well, as certain as I am of anything, but perhaps nothing is as I see it, perhaps I am not standing in a room in O—— Street, in a house in Moscow, and that is not Severine who is reading in a chair by the stove. Perhaps—but what is the good of wondering.

December 3rd.

More shadows that seemed to twist about and grow and shrink up on the wall. I could see them after I had put the light out too. No sleep again.

This afternoon I walked into the public gardens. The sky was pale blue and the air was mild. The sun shone steadily. Round the garden there is a gravel path separated from the road by a low iron palisade. Over this I could see into the road as I sank into one of the seats that are placed at intervals along the skirts of the gardens.

How my eyes ached with sleeplessness. I could hear the roar of the traffic around me. Every one had turned out to enjoy the air. Carriages whirled past with tall, handsome women in them, and I heard the crack of whips and the curious jerking cries of the coachmen urging on their horses.

I took off my hat and felt the warm sun upon my hair. My eyes dropped from the sight of the busy traffic upon the yellow gravel.

Gradually the cries of the coachmen and the rattling of the wheels became mingled into one dull roar, then I forgot that this noise was caused by horses and whips and people. I began to wonder where I was, and almost to feel a kind of wonder as to what I was. The houses and the shops, and the trees in the gardens, all faded into a mist, and I found my eyes riveted on two flies that circled round each other on the sunlit gravel path. Sometimes one rested for a moment and then the other collided with it, and off they went again, circling round and round and round, and they seemed to be the chief characters in the scene round me. Everything else had faded away into the background.

I began to speculate on how long they would go on flying round and round, and which would stop first. Then I forgot altogether that they were flies, and only saw a patch of yellow and two tiny black specks revolving in it.

I suppose I must have slept a little on the seat. I felt cold as I picked up my hat and walked home. The sun had gone in behind heavy grey clouds, and the roar of the traffic seemed to be deeper than it was before.

December 4th.

My fan has been found in a drawer. I am positive that I never put it there.

Last night I dreamed I was under water.

For some time I did not sink to the bottom, and then I began to drop down, down, down, such a long way, until I felt my face touch a glutinous clay which seemed to suck me in, and my hair was waving above me in the water-like long reeds. Then my body seemed to grow into the clay, and I became unconscious of everything but the long reeds pulling from the roots now this way, now that.

December 9th.

To-morrow night my work is to be performed to the public. The excitement is tremendous : all the tickets have been sold, the papers have all talked of it as the event of the year. The poet has addressed an ode to me in a volume of verses that have just been published. Musicians have come from Paris, Vienna, Milan, and London. Severine says it will be a triumph. The next day we are to go into the country to rest.

What do I care about the next day? Perhaps I shall not be here to know the next day. But I shall have made thousands wonder at the work of one. How they will hang on every note. I shall watch them as the performance goes on. I will creep round amongst the audience and listen, to hear if they are restless or so absorbed that they do not move a muscle.

December 10th.

How the time drags. I wish the evening were here. I have sat for hours gazing at the shadow creeping over the white house opposite. The sun shines so steadily and brightly. How slowly the shadow grows. The room is full of light; everything stands out equally boldly. And there is a long shaft of dust caught up by the sun that cuts right across.

Let me try and think what dress I shall wear to-night. I think it shall be the old one in which I went to the Lorrimers' dance: the last time I wore it was when I went to Severine that night in August.

My father and mother cannot have found out where I am. They will not aid in my triumph to-night. I should have liked them to be there. We might have understood each other better afterwards.

How the sun bores me with its steady penetrating beams.

I can see them again sitting opposite each other in the drawing-room. The same scene over and over again. I wish I could get rid of the thought of it. The same merciless smile on the lips of the portrait at six years old.

All the people are back in the square now, and there has been whispering and scandal talked about me, and there must be many who shake their heads and say 'I told you so, I always fancied,' and the men will ridicule and laugh, and my name will be on their coarse brutal lips when they sit alone and the women have left them. Why should I be blamed for defying a society like this?

How quiet it must be in the old house! Never thes ound of the piano. Perhaps the blinds in my room have been pulled down. The room must be very dark. I can see the piles of music in the corner, covered with a thick layer of dust, and the old picture of Beethoven over the mantelpiece, and the ebony piano by the window, and a tall glass full of shrivelled flowers and discoloured water. When I left I told the servants not to touch the room until I returned, as there were papers of importance lying about and bits of manuscript.

Perhaps they are keeping the room just as it is to await my return. Or perhaps they think I am dead, and that is why the blinds have been pulled down. I wish I had not left those flowers. I cannot bear to think of them in their shrivelled state. They have withered since I left—and I? I, too, have withered. I am not so beautiful as I was, and yet the young poet tells me that every day I grow more lovely.

He writes me verses. The other day he showed me some. There was one line that struck me:

'And all her beauty fled into her eyes.'

Yes, the body is losing its shape and the face is growing thin and white, but the eyes grow larger and there is a strange look in them.

. . . .

Only half an hour to wait now and then we start. I have spent at least two hours over dressing.

I cannot grasp the fact that what I am going to hear is all my own work, and that I am responsible for it. Now that it is complete and ready for criticism, it seems to me to belong to another person.

They have brought me a long trail of white

roses for my dress. As I pinned them on, I felt that I was decking a corpse and my hands trembled so that I could scarcely fix them in their place. Then Severine came in and said I must wear one in my hair. So he detached one from the trail and fixed it in with a hair-pin. As he was trying to arrange it I thought of

> 'Lilies for a bridal bed,
> Roses for a matron's head.'

I might have been spared the remembrance of these lines; and then I saw the 'Madonna' face at Dinard, the woman in her simple dark dress, and I could have torn mine to shreds.

. . . .

I hear him calling. It is time for us to go.

December 11th. 1 a.m.

Something is going round at lightning speed, and beating against the sides of my head. It is useless to try and sleep.

What crowds of carriages there were. Yes, it has been a triumph, but I cannot forget the great face. How horrible it was.

They performed magnificently, and I crept

round amongst the audience and listened to hear if they moved, but they remained absolutely still.

Before we began, I saw the crowds pouring in and Severine pointed out numbers of distinguished people. Then, when the signal was given, the brilliant lights were all turned out at once, and we commenced on the stage behind our curtain.

They never performed so well. Not a hitch the whole time.

It lasted about two hours. I had given instructions for the lights to be turned up as soon as the last note was finished. I have never been so absorbed as while it was going on. I completely forgot my surroundings. At times I felt as if I were in a forest which was peopled with gigantic trees whose branches were so thickly interwoven that scarcely any light could penetrate. And I heard the rushing of a mighty cataract, and then the tops of the trees dissolved and a flood of dazzling light poured in.

. . . .

Just before the last few bars the white rose fell from my hair and I became conscious of where I was. Without stopping to pick it up,

I stepped to the curtain and gazed through a small opening in it.

In another moment the lights burst out all over the theatre as the last note sounded.

As I looked I saw nothing but one huge immovable face which filled all the theatre. It was colossal, and the mouth wore a terrifying smile. . . .

I gazed spellbound at this colossal thing, . . . then suddenly a corruption seemed to seize the flesh, and every particle began to move and twist about. I felt as if my brain was giving way. The sudden life that burst over this inert mass filled me with such a horror that I turned my eyes away and gasped for breath. At the same time a roar of voices deafened my ears. It grew louder and louder, until I felt some one touch me. It was Severine who said to me in an excited voice — his eyes dancing with enthusiasm—

'They want you—you must make your bow.'

I scarcely understood what he said, but he led me to the side of the stage, and then gently pushed me in front of the curtain.

Still that awful corruption. Now it was working more rapidly. There was a shout of applause from every corner in the building, and I tottered off. But they began again, first it was softer, and then it grew and grew until I was told I must appear again, but I refused. Over and over again the noise swelled and subsided in anticipation of my reappearance. But I could not look upon that awful face again. So I said I was dead with fatigue and some one must speak an excuse for me.

I had sunk into a chair at the side of the stage. The noise had now reached its highest. The conductor of the orchestra went on and there was a sudden hush. I could not hear him speak, but in a few moments the applause began again until it grew into a great shout mixed with the stamping of feet. Then it gradually subsided, and I could hear the noise of the people leaving the great theatre.

I was overcome by an intense weariness. I closed my eyes and the whole scene seemed to slip away, and again I was in the wood with the gigantic trees; but they did not leave me alone. Crowds of distinguished musicians had come on to the stage for an introduction. There was a chorus of congratulations in the air mingled with the clatter of horses' hoofs on the paved street outside, and the cries of the coachmen which came in through the opened doors.

Then Severine came to me and whispered that some one wanted an introduction—a great man. I just caught the name of Tolstoi, and I dimly remember a massive figure with a broad forehead, from which the iron grey hair was brushed back over the temples. There was a look of generous enthusiasm in the deepset brilliant grey eyes which flashed from under shaggy brows.

Then I fainted. When I was sufficiently well to go, the house had become empty, but there was still a considerable sound of confusion from outside. I came out on Severine's arm, and the air was cool and refreshing to my heated face.

There was a lurid light over everything. A hundred flaming torches were smoking and burning fiercely in different places. As soon as I came out there was a cry which was caught up by the torch-bearers. At the same time I felt a number of soft leaves beat against my face and neck. They were flowers which the crowd were throwing. I shuddered slightly and passed along. Then the torch-bearers formed a procession and accompanied us home, singing the national songs and shouting.

What is the good of such a triumph? The remembrance of that face will never leave me.

December 19*th.*

I was too ill the day after the performance to go into the country. I have been in bed ever since. Sometimes my brain wanders, but the score of my work has never left me for a moment. I hear every note of it from beginning to end over and over again.

From my bed I can see through the window down into the street.

The world is like a great poem that has been written to my music. So it seems to me as I look at the houses and the sky and the people passing to and fro, while the music is ringing in my ears.

The pattern in the sky changes. Clouds flit across the blue. They split up into fantastic shapes. Every second there is a change; the light in the street changes; . . . the figures traced by the people always moving change; so, too, there are changes in my music.

At times the houses and the people and the sky lose their meaning for me. I gaze helplessly at them. They seem to express something, but I cannot find out what. So, too, my music expresses something which I cannot fix in my mind. And I cannot stop thinking till my head is ready to burst.

. . . . . .

December 21st.

Still my music pursues me. It maddens me. I can see nothing and I can feel nothing, but my ears are full of music growing louder and louder.

. . . . . .
. . . . . .
. . . . . .

Why have they shut me up here? What have I done? They have taken everything from me. They tell me I am ill, and that I must keep quiet for a long time. But I am not more ill than I have always been. When I was born I must have been what they call 'ill.' But why did they bring me here? Why couldn't I stay in the house where Severine——

I cannot remember. After the performance I was ill—yes, I remember that, and I went to bed, and then—there is a gap that I cannot fill up. The next thing I remember is being carried down the stairs, and put into a carriage with two women both dressed exactly alike, and then a long, long drive. That is all. But just before we started, I think Severine talked to the two women at the door, and it was about me; but he never said good-bye to me. He seemed to look upon me as a stranger, and I was too weak to ask him about it, and I felt sleepy and only half conscious of what was going on around me. Now I am stronger, but still they keep me a prisoner here.

Bare walls, in one of which is a recess with cushions for my bed I suppose. A chair, a table, pen and ink. It was good of them to leave me these. But why have they locked the door and bolted the window from outside?

How untidy I feel. My hair is all loose and straggling. I want a glass and a brush. My dress is torn too. Who tore my dress? Who—

My head is beginning to ache and that fear is coming over me.

How bright the sunlight is. It follows me about. There is not a corner in the room where it does not pursue me.

THE MIRROR OF MUSIC

Outside far down below my window stretches flat, open country. I cannot see a house anywhere. Close to my window are a few tall naked trees, their topmost branches just reach to my window.

. . . .

My head is full of music, music—always music. Why is it all so quiet in this house? I cannot hear a sound. I want to hear something else but this music. Where is everybody?

How dreary the landscape looks. And that merciless sun, how it shines on! I hear footsteps, footsteps—yes, coming towards my door. . . .

It was a man in dark clothes with a light blue patch on his left sleeve embroidered with some sign. He asked me if I wanted anything to eat. I told him that all I wanted was a looking-glass and a brush and comb. He has gone away again. Perhaps I am in a hospital and he is the attendant. I think I shall try and sleep a little.

The sun is setting. How still it is. Not a creature for miles. But in the distance there is a row of naked poplars. Sometimes I fancy they lean towards my window, and then bend slowly back. No other motion over the wide stretch of land outside my window.

Still music, music. As I look out of the window I seem to hear it in a lower key. . . .

The attendant has been in again, but he has not brought me a looking-glass.

I should like to write to my mother to come to me. Perhaps if she saw me she would forgive me. Since I have been ill I have forgotten even the address of my home, and nothing can recall it to me. I have puzzled for hours, but it only makes my head ache. What does it matter? I don't think I can last very long.

The next morning.

Last night I heard the melody of 'Aveu.' I did not dare open my eyes for fear I should see the figure by my bedside. But I dreamed of a spring night in a garden with the dew upon the grass: and the moonlight, calm and white. And far away I heard the sob of a woman full of an intense grief. It mingled with the liquid note of a nightingale. And there was a throbbing life in the young buds of the shrubs. I could almost feel the pulse

THE MIRROR OF MUSIC

beating in them. They seemed to be sucking the life from the woman who cried. Her voice grew weaker and weaker until it ceased. Then the moonbeams seemed to grow brighter, and the twigs to stretch out with fresh vigour, . . . and the melody ceased and I awoke.

All day I have sat at my window and looked out. There is a high wind. The sky is cloudy and dull. At wide intervals there are groups of short stubbly trees that quiver with the buffets of the wind. In the distance miles and miles away, thin, black stems of tall poplars are bowing to me every moment. There is sound to-day, the sound of the wind sweeping over the earth which seems to moan with its chill touch.

Just now a bird flew against the window-pane and flapped with its wings. I tried to open it to let it in, but it was closed fast from outside and in a moment the poor little thing fell to the ground—dead, I suppose.

Evening now. Soft flakes brush against the window. They are covering up the little feathered body that lies below.

Still music, music, music.

Outside all is covered with white.

On the surface of the earth I see a woman's shape—huge, and stretching for miles. She lies with face upturned. Her feet are towards me. The white robe is over her. I see the gentle curve of her enormous breasts. They glisten white in the sun. I cannot see her face. But I know that her eyes are looking at me, and that they bid me come to her.

Last night as I lay on my bed the music which I hear in my head stopped. There was perfect stillness, and I knew that the figure in white was beside me. Then, as if it came from miles away, I heard a woman's voice. She was speaking to me.

'You are sailing towards the island of music: I will be your guide, for the waters are dark. When you have touched the land the sun shall shine for you.'

'Sit at your window and watch till the pictures of life rise before you. To each picture there shall be music and the world shall be unfolded to you.'

Then the voice died away.

And now again I see the glistening form of

the woman in the snow-clad earth and I am waiting, waiting at my window.

. . . .

What did it all mean? I cannot tell. Yet soon I shall know, for, did not the voice tell me that I was sailing to the island of music? Yes, soon, soon, the sun will shine for me.

* * * * * * *

Outside, the fields were covered with human figures and there was the sound of music in the air.

In the middle stood a Tower. It stretched right up to the sky, passing even through the clouds, so that to those below the summit was shrouded in darkness.

The figure in white touched me and we passed out into the fields.

Here were great tumult and confusion in the crowd. So, too, there was confusion in the sounds that I heard. And the people pushed and struggled this way and that, and some fell, for the crowd was great, and they could not battle through.

But round the Tower was an open space and no one had penetrated here.

So we passed along, and the crowd seemed to melt before us as we went, so that there was a path for us. Soon we came to the open space and the tumult grew faint in my ears. Then we stood at the base of the Tower and the figure in white pointed upwards. So we began to ascend.

And as I touched the Tower a marvellous melody sounded in my ears—clear and pure. Higher and higher I climbed and the melody grew higher and higher.

Now I turned to look down and dimly I saw the tumult of figures like a cloud of insects.

Higher and higher again I mounted until I passed through the clouds. The light around me was dazzling and the melody was singing in my ears high and clear.

And I beheld a builder toiling at the summit of the Tower, and his eyes were filled with a strange radiance. And as he put the crowning piece to his work, I heard the music of the melody higher and clearer than before.

Then he tottered and fell to the earth and the figure in white bade me follow.

So we sank swiftly to the ground, and as we sank, the music of the melody died away. And we crossed the open space to the fields, where there was the tumult of the people.

THE MIRROR OF MUSIC

Now the clouds above dispersed for a moment and the people beheld the summit of the tower, and around it the dazzling light, and they shouted and waved their hands, for they knew that the builder's work was of marvellous beauty; and a sound came to them:

It was like a great cry from afar.

Then the clouds gathered again about the tower, and all was tumult and confusion as before.

* * * * * * *

Most of the snow outside has cleared away, but here and there are white patches.

The attendant has been to see me again. He is the only human being I see now. He has not brought me a looking-glass. I grew very angry and threatened to kill myself if he would not bring me one. I will see myself: it will be so exciting to see if I am much changed. He has gone away to fetch me one. My hair feels very untidy. I will brush it before he comes back, and set my dress straight, that I may look my best when the glass comes. . . .

I hear his footsteps. He is coming. I am all in a tremble. How shall I look? Shall I recognise my features?

I am alone with the glass. I don't like to look at it now. It is lying face downwards beside me as I write. It has an ivory back and a monogram embossed in tarnished silver. I wonder whose it can be. It cannot belong to the hospital. Perhaps it has been borrowed from a patient.

The doors here must be very heavily padded. I never hear the sound of anybody next to me. Perhaps I am in a wing by myself. . . .

Still it lies by my side, and somehow I would rather go on writing than take it up. I can see it in the hands of some pretty woman dressed for a ball, she is standing by a large mirror and holding this little oval glass in front of her face. Her back is opposite the large glass. She has turned round in a sweeping curve which joins the daintily poised head. A small white hand is pinning a jewel in the back of her hair. She has just fixed it and has turned to contemplate the reflection of her pretty features in the small oval glass. An almost imperceptible smile flits over her face.

Why should I think of this?

At first I did not recognise myself. I only saw a shrunken head from which masses of hair straggled, and instinctively I crushed the hair together and twisted it with my other hand. It looked top-heavy: the face was too slender to bear so much. Then I saw a white skin marked with a web of blue veins, and here and there black patches.

It took me a long time to recognise fully that it was my own face that was reflected. Then a great pain seemed to stifle me for a moment. Can those great staring eyes be mine? And I was beautiful once too. But, of course, I have been ill: I could not expect that there would be no traces of it on my face. And then as I looked it seemed to me that the reflection was only a small part of myself, and I began to think.

Yes, it was my body that I saw reflected; its form and colour, but again I seemed to want to see a meaning behind it. As it was, it represented only one of the many things that I saw in the world. The pattern on the wall was reflected too. Both reflections seemed to be of equal importance to me, but I felt that I in my entirety was something much more than the glass could show me.

And then the melody of the music from the Tower, broken and indistinct, came into my head, and, without knowing why, I let my hand fall from the hair that I had been tightening.

I do not know what day it is, but the spring is beginning. I can tell it from the few trees that are close to my window. Everything is beginning to throb with a new life, while I feel as I did on that night when I could not sleep, and the birds began to chirp and twitter in the early dawn. But I must not despair. Am I not sailing to the island of music—through the darkness of the waters to the light?

There is something strange about the twilight now. It is so subtle and the light fades away so mysteriously. I sit at the window and watch for the last gleam of the sun, and then I look, and look, until absolute darkness covers everything. I don't like to let any single object out of my sight, so I strain my eyes to keep its shape as long as I can. At this time of the day the broken melody haunts me most persistently. It seems to have grown hard and frozen as when a liquid crystallises, and the spars shoot in different directions, making patterns on what was before a liquid surface.

The figure in white is guiding me.

* * * * * * *

O mother, how red the sun looks to-night! Fierce shafts shoot up from the west, and the glowing ball is crowned with a sullen grey cloud. The stillness of the air is broken only by the chattering of the birds. How restlessly they flutter round the bough of the tree near my window. There is no movement in the fields. Far away in the horizon I see my row of poplars shiver occasionally.

The black cloud over the sun is distorting itself into fantastic shapes, but it clings to the great red ball. Now it is a tree with great black branches that stretch towards my window, and now it is a monstrous bird with wings that stretch far on either side.

The sun is nearly set, but the cloud still

changes, though its outline is becoming dimmer and dimmer every moment, and now the shape is of an enormous monkey. I can see the curve of his great back and the long arms. How colossal he seems in the dull dead coloured twilight. Only a few faint gleams of reddish gold are to be seen now. . . .

It is dark and still I can see the shape of that monkey, and music is ringing in my ears.

. . . .

How they climb about! A forest of trees has sprung up. They are scantily clad. I can see the monkeys twisting in and out of the branches. Their green eyes flash. Wherever I look I see them. They have peopled the whole space. Some squat on the ground and grin. And some swing from the branches by their tails. There are a few that are enormous —as tall as the trees, and they have great hairy bodies; . . . but most of them are smaller, some quite tiny, . . . and they herd together in families, . . . and there are sounds in the air confused and inconsequent; but there is no melody like the music from the Tower, only one note sounds through all. The other sounds change sometimes into shrieks, and then into a

THE MIRROR OF MUSIC

dull roar, and then into a flat hard sound, but the tone of this note is constant :

The other sounds all cluster round it and melt into it. And the monkeys still climb and twist about. . . . No melody, no melody: only this one note.

* * * * * * *

All night I have watched and still the same sound has been in my ears. Now the dawn is breaking. The shapes are growing vague and shadowy. I press my face against the pane to try and see them still, but they are slipping away. A cold dull light is stealing over the earth. I begin to see a hedge. Before, it was full of shapes, but now they seem gathered up, and though I try to see them still, the shape of the hedge obtrudes itself upon me, the network of brown twigs emerges from the darkness. And now there is a stream of light in the sky, and all the million shapes seem gathered into a great grey cloud that hangs over the head of the sun as he rolls up from the horizon.

The stems of my poplars are like thin black lines against a background of gold. The sounds have sunk into a whisper, and I can only hear that one note faintly.

What this one note means I cannot make out. There is something in it that I can no more explain than the something which made me drop my hand from the hair which I had tightened when I looked at myself in the glass.

I am tired of thinking, thinking. Am I nearer to the island? I think I am, but still it is dark, and I cannot guess the meaning of the things which I have seen.

No one comes to see me. It seems as if there was no one else in the world but myself. I am alone with my creations, these pictures that I see. Well, they are no more phantasies than what other people see. Oh! when will it end? But I want to know the meaning of it. It has a meaning, it must have. . . .

I want a toy to play with, one like those I had when I was a child, a little horse with rough bristling hair and a grey and white body. I will hold it in my hand and think that I am very fond of it as I used to, . . . when my mother . . . I think I have killed her. She is dying with grief because . . . but I could not help it—don't die, mother, don't die.

There is a tiny blossom on the tree near my window. I can see it grow day by day. The landscape is becoming green. The sun is warmer.

Soon, soon the secret will be mine. The figure is guiding me to the island of discovery where there is light. . . .

* * * * * * *

It was the same scene as before, but the trees were covered with leaves.

There was the sound of rushing water and the sun blazed fiercely on everything.

A strong wind swept over the ground which was covered with animals.

The figure in white guided me among them.

And as I walked, a sound burst from the wood and my body trembled and gave out a deep note that seemed to vibrate all over me. I felt savage, and like some wild beast tried to gnaw at the bark of a tree. And then the water sounded in my ears like a fierce cataract, the wind groaned, and all these sounds melted into the note which seemed to come from my body:

And then it was as if a cold damp sheet flapped against me until I moved and found myself again in my room, and I knew that the figure was by me.

So I gazed from my window and saw that the trees had grown thicker, and the animals that peopled the wood were of monstrous size, and still I heard a deep sound, deeper than that which came from me before, and the note that sounded through it all was this:—

Then the whole picture faded from my eyes and all I saw, after gazing for a long time in front of me, was the blossom on the tree near my window.

At first I thought that it had grown to an enormous flower that covered all the landscape, then it began to shrink and grow smaller and smaller, until I saw it in its original size on the tree.

* * * * * * *

The sounds descend at each picture that I see and the melody from the Tower has never returned. The world is being unfolded to me from the supremacy of man back to . . . Who can tell? And the music follows.

Nearer still to the great meaning. But I am weak and fear, that before I reach the island, I shall die, and still the great secret will remain undisclosed. . . . I will pray for strength in case there be a god or power of some sort to help me. . . . Only for a time, for when it is reached then the earth may take me.

To-day I thought I saw the great blossom again, stretching over the expanse outside my window, and as I looked, it broke into fields on fields of brilliant flowers. They were of many colours and quivered in the sunlight. And there were clouds of bees and butterflies and insects that swarmed over them, and the air was full of a pungent perfume, . . . but the figure was not with me. I heard no sound and I knew that there was no meaning in the picture. It flashed before me in a second and then died away. . . .

Just now a half starved looking cat crept along

under my window. How strange it is that in all animals there is the same scheme: head, nose, eyes, mouth, legs, and trunk. I feel as if there were not, perhaps after all, so much difference between me and that creeping thing. I watched it just now. It moved on a few paces—stopped, looked round, and then crept under a hedge at which it clutched first with one uplifted paw—to see if it was full of prickles, I suppose—and now it lies with its head upwards and the hungry green eyes stare at me out of the thin head in which they are set.

I know its feeling so well. The lean hollow body covered with miserable hairs, and the lifeless tail all limp. And the cold touch of the earth on which it lies.

* * * * * * *

Again the shadow is by me. The surface of the earth is naked and the air is clear, and there is a great light as of a million suns.

The surface of the earth seems to move. Huge reptiles creep and writhe. They stretch over vast expanses, and, as I gaze at their bodies that sweep about in immense curves, the shadow seems to have come nearer to me and I hear the sound of a deep note:

THE MIRROR OF MUSIC

* * * * * * *

And then I felt the touch of the figure in white, and we floated out into the dazzling air until from above where we were poised the shadow pointed down.

And below us lay a vast expanse of clear liquid in which strange fish of different shapes swam about. And their colours were many, and the sound of the note was still in my ears, but sometimes it sank to this:

* * * * * * *

And when I was again in my room I felt that the island was nearly reached.

Still, as yet, the meaning of all these sounds is hidden from me. They have followed me through these pictures. I have seen and heard: yet out of the whole, I can find no single meaning. There is still a secret to unravel. Since the beginning the sounds have descended, but together the phrase does not explain itself.

There is a sequence in the sounds for they form a chord, and the additional note to come will be another one in the harmony of the chord. Yet it is a minor chord, and I hear no solution to it. And there seems no meaning to be gathered from the scenes that have passed before my eyes, except that they go further and further back from the supremacy of man.

The air is stifling. Outside the grass is being scorched by the burning sun. There is the hum of insects. I can see them swarming in the petals of the bloom on the tree outside my window. It is as if they generated thousands in a second. Every moment the middle of the flower grows blacker with them.

In the distance I see a tree with a thin stem, at the top of which the foliage is so thick that it looks almost as if it were in one piece. Just now I thought I saw a thin face beneath this crown of hair. It reminded me of the face I saw in the glass that was brought to me some time ago. I dare not look at it again.

How my eyes ache! The fields look parched with thirst. For weeks there has been no rain, and the sky is clear to-day. No sign of showers to come. I have waited through long nights for the figure in white, but it has left me for a long time now. Perhaps, after all, I shall never know the great secret, and yet, if not, why have I seen those pictures?

A few nights ago when the sky was covered with brilliant stars I thought that swarms of black insects clustered round and crept over them as over the bloom on the tree, and gradually the whole sky was black and I waited for the figure; but it did not come, and the sun rose and dispelled the darkness, and I began to wonder at the coming of a new day.

Oh, I am tired, so tired of watching. My limbs ache, and my body has grown thin. I can feel the lines as I pass my hand across my face. My beauty has fled and my life is drifting away as in my dream of the girl who cried so bitterly in that garden in the spring until her voice died away in the note of a nightingale, and the twigs of the shrubs stretched forth and the moonbeams grew brighter.

* * * * * * *

The figure is beside me: again there is a forest.

The trees are huge and thick with leaves of a million kinds. They stretch up to the sky and the branches weave in and out of each other. There are woods upon woods.

The light of the sun is shut out from above by the leaves.

From the side pours in a dim light. I see the tall black stems. They shoot up miles high and the earth is covered with plants of a million shapes. They twine in and out of each other, and the roots of the trees spread far amongst them.

There is a strong smell of earth. And over all, a dead silence.

And I can feel the life in the growing plants. They cannot generate quickly enough. Every moment that I look, some new plant seemed to have pushed its way up from the earth.

And ever the same mighty stillness. And the plants neither see, nor hear, nor speak. They know nothing but the desire to live. . . .

The figure is beside me; we do not float out into the scene as before. I am straining my ears to catch a sound, but I hear nothing but the stillness.

. . . .

Then I turned aside as if to question the figure, but it only made a sign for me to listen

THE MIRROR OF MUSIC

and to look. So I turned again to the window and it seemed that the air had grown denser, and that the trees were taller, and the plants thicker, and I listened, I seemed to listen for years, then I heard a very faint sound. It seemed to come with great effort. I had only just time to catch the note before it died away :

* * * * * * *

Closer still to the island. A light begins to dawn upon me. Soon, soon I shall know the secret.

I begin to think that all the story of my life has been a dream and that I have only just woke up and found that all the people I have known so long were mere fancies created by my brain. The one living thing for me has been music, the rest were phantoms.

Where is the figure in white?

I must know the meaning of it all. I am close to land. I can hear the music of the water breaking on the shore of my island, but I cannot reach the land alone. Perhaps I shall never reach it. Have they put a barrier before me, and am I to beat helplessly against it, like the bird outside my window?

The history of life has been unfolded to me from the supremacy of man back to the dawn of life in plants. What comes next?

* * * * * * *

I think I hear the crash of planets, millions of ages ago when the world was formed.

After this there is a time when there is no life, but all is dull, heavy mass. It is the age of granite. Listen! There is sound to this too. Yes, the figure in white is helping me.

It is a heavy bass sound far deeper and more difficult to move than any of the sounds I have heard before. It is impossible even to imagine a sound so deep.

* * * * * * *

Alone in my island now. The sun shines for me.

I have come across the darkness of the waters to the land where there is light.

The figure in white is by my side, and the air is full of song, a wild beautiful song, and the melody is the music from the Tower, and the words are these:—

'There is a great mirror made of bright metal
'Outside it is a mighty power.
'The reflection of the power in the mirror—is the world.
'And the influence of the power on the mirror draws sound from the metal, and this is music.
'The reflection depends not on the sound, nor the sound on the reflection.
'But both depend on the power.
'And the power depends on nothing: for it is absolute.
'You have heard the melody of the music from the Tower. It came from that part of the mirror wherein was reflected the highest form of life.
'For to the builder the essence of the power was revealed, as now it is revealed to you.
'The world is made up of many things.
'There are sun and moon and stars.
'There are land and water and living creatures, and countless other things. And they are to one another as the notes in a great piece of music.
'It is vain to seek a meaning in the world: it is vain to seek a meaning in music.

'The sound of rushing water is beautiful. Yet who shall account for it by reason?

'The world has been unfolded to you, and you know its beauty.

'It is a great poem:

'And there is music to it: a chord in the minor.

'And the chord is unresolved.'

* * * * * * *

This was the song that sounded in the air.

How the dew dances in the sunlight of the early morning. There is joy in the chorus of the birds, and the wind is soft and fresh, and there is a deep content in my heart.

For I stand at the summit of my Tower like the builder ... and I listen to the music of the melody, and look out on the world. And the air is free and light.

I am ready to die now, for I have laboured, ... and a child has been born to me. Its name is Truth.

* * * *
 * * *
  * *
   *

Here the diary ended. At the foot of the last

THE MIRROR OF MUSIC

page were a few pencil notes in Severine's handwriting. They consisted chiefly of references to Schopenhauer and Wagner. There was also a phrase quoted from Beethoven, op. 57.

By the side of it was written this note in French, signed with the initials 'S. M.'

Here is the passage that came into Sarah Kaftal's head, note by note when she saw the pictures from her window: but the notes occurred to her in the inverse order, so that she did not recognise their source.

Printed by T. and A. CONSTABLE, Printers to Her Majesty
at the Edinburgh University Press

John Lane
The Bodley Head
VIGO STREET, LONDON, W.

THE KEYNOTES SERIES.

Crown 8vo, cloth. Each volume with a Title-page and Cover Design by AUBREY BEARDSLEY. 3s. 6d. net.

 I. KEYNOTES. By GEORGE EGERTON. Seventh Edition.
 II. THE DANCING FAUN. By FLORENCE FARR.
 III. POOR FOLK. By FEDOR DOSTOIEVSKY. Translated from the Russian by LENA MILMAN. With an Introduction by GEORGE MOORE.
 IV. A CHILD OF THE AGE. By FRANCIS ADAMS.
 V. THE GREAT GOD PAN AND THE INMOST LIGHT. By ARTHUR MACHEN. Second Edition.
 VI. DISCORDS. By GEORGE EGERTON. Fourth Edition.
 VII. PRINCE ZALESKI. By M. P. SHIEL.
 VIII. THE WOMAN WHO DID. By GRANT ALLEN. Sixteenth Edition.
 IX. WOMEN'S TRAGEDIES. By H. D. LOWRY.
 X. GREY ROSES. By HENRY HARLAND.
 XI. AT THE FIRST CORNER, AND OTHER STORIES. By H. B. MARRIOTT WATSON.
 XII. MONOCHROMES. By ELLA D'ARCY.
 XIII. AT THE RELTON ARMS. By EVELYN SHARP.
 XIV. THE GIRL FROM THE FARM. By GERTRUDE DIX.
 XV. THE MIRROR OF MUSIC. By STANLEY V. MAKOWER.
 XVI. YELLOW AND WHITE. By W. CARLTON DAWE.
 XVII. THE MOUNTAIN LOVERS. By FIONA MACLEOD.
 XVIII. THE THREE IMPOSTORS. By ARTHUR MACHEN.
 [*In preparation.*

Copyright Editions of the volumes of the KEYNOTES SERIES are published in the United States by Messrs. ROBERTS BROS. of Boston.

Seventh Edition, now ready.

KEYNOTES. By GEORGE EGERTON. With Title-page by AUBREY BEARDSLEY. Crown 8vo, cloth, 3s. 6d. net.

'Emboldened, doubtless, by the success of "Dodo," the author of "Keynotes" offers us a set of stories written with the least amount of literary skill and in the worst literary taste. We have refrained from quotation, for fear of giving to this book an importance which it does not merit.'—*Pall Mall Gazette.*

'The sirens sing in it from the first page to the last. It may, perhaps, shock you with disregard of conventionality and reticencies, but you will all the same have to admit its fascination. There can be no doubt that in Mr. George Egerton his publishers have discovered a story-teller of genius. —*Star.*

'This is a collection of eight of the prettiest short stories that have appeared for many a day. They turn for the most part on feminine traits of character; in fact, the book is a little psychological study of woman under various circumstances. The characters are so admirably drawn, and the scenes and landscapes are described with so much and so rare vividness, that one cannot help being almost spell-bound by their perusal.'—*St. James's Gazette.*

'A rich, passionate temperament vibrates through every line. . . . We have met nothing so lovely in its tenderness since Mr. Kipling's "Without Benefit of Clergy."'—*Daily Chronicle.*

'For any one who cares more for truth than for orthodox mummery, and for the real flood of the human heart than for the tepid negus which stirs the veins of respectability, this little book deserves a hearty welcome.' —*Sketch.*

'Singularly artistic in its brilliant suggestiveness.'—*Daily News.*

'This is a book which is a portentous sign of our times. The wildness, the fierceness, the animality that underlie the soft, smooth surface of woman's pretty and subdued face—this is the theme to which she again and again recurs.'—T. P. in *Weekly Sun.*

'To credit a new writer with the possession of genius is a serious matter, but it is nevertheless a verdict which Mr. George Egerton can hardly avoid at the hands of those who read his delightful sketches.'—*Liverpool Post.*

'These lovely sketches are informed by such throbbing feeling, such insight into complex woman, that we with all speed and warmth advise those who are in search of splendid literature to procure "Keynotes" without delay.'—*Literary World.*

'These very clever stories of Mr. Egerton's.'—*Black and White.*

'The reading of it is an adventure, and, once begun, it is hard to tear yourself from the book till you have devoured every line. There is impulsive life in every word of it. It has passion, ardour, vehement romance. It is full of youth; often enough the revolt and despair of youth.'—*Irish Independent.*

'Every line of the book gives the impression that here some woman has crystallised her life's drama; has written down her soul upon the page. — *Review of Reviews.*

'The work of a woman who has lived every hour of her life, be she young or old. . . . She allows us, like the great artists of old, Shakespeare and Goethe, to draw our own moral from the stories she tells, and it is with no uncertain touch or faltering hand that she pulls aside the curtain of conventional hypocrisy which hundreds of women hang between the world and their own hearts. . . . The insight of the writer into the curious and complicated nature of women is almost miraculous.'—*Lady's Pictorial.*

'Not since the "Story of an African Farm" was written has any woman delivered herself of so strong, so forcible a book.'—*Queen.*

'She is a writer with a profound understanding of the human heart. She understands men; and, more than this, she understands women. ... For those who weary of the conventional fiction, and who long for something out of the ordinary run of things, these are tales that carry the zest of living.'—*Boston Beacon.*

'It is not a book for babes and sucklings, since it cuts deep into rather dangerous soil; but it is refined and skilful ... strikes a very true and touching note of pathos.'—*Westminster Gazette.*

'The author of these able word sketches is manifestly a close observer of Nature's moods, and one, moreover, who carefully takes stock of the up-to-date thoughts that shake mankind.'—*Daily Telegraph.*

'Powerful pictures of human beings living to-day, full of burning pain, and thought, and passion.'—*Bookman.*

'A work of genius. There is upon the whole thing a stamp of down-right inevitableness as of things which must be written, and written exactly in that way.'—*Speaker.*

'"Keynotes" is a singularly clever book.'—*Truth.*

THE DANCING FAUN. By FLORENCE FARR. With Title-page and Cover Design by AUBREY BEARDSLEY. Crown 8vo, 3s. 6d. net.

'We welcome the light and merry pen of Miss Farr as one of the deftest that has been wielded in the style of to-day. She has written the cleverest and the most cynical sensation story of the season.'—*Liverpool Daily Post.*

'Slight as it is, the story is, in its way, strong.'—*Literary World.*

'Full of bright paradox, and paradox which is no mere topsy-turvy play upon words, but the product of serious thinking upon life. One of the cleverest of recent novels.'—*Star.*

'It is full of epigrammatic effects, and it has a certain thread of pathos calculated to win our sympathy.'—*Queen.*

'The story is subtle and psychological after the fashion of modern psychology; it is undeniably clever and smartly written.'—*Gentlewoman.*

'No one can deny its freshness and wit. Indeed there are things in it here and there which John Oliver Hobbes herself might have signed without loss of reputation.'—*Woman.*

'There is a lurid power in the very unreality of the story. One does not quite understand how Lady Geraldine worked herself up to shooting her lover, but when she has done it, the description of what passes through her mind is magnificent.'—*Athenæum.*

'Written by an obviously clever woman.'—*Black and White.*

'Miss Farr has talent. "The Dancing Faun" contains writing that is distinctively good. Doubtless it is only a prelude to something much stronger.'—*Academy.*

'As a work of art the book has the merit of brevity and smart writing; while the *dénouement* is skilfully prepared, and comes as a surprise. If the book had been intended as a satire on the "new woman" sort of literature, it would have been most brilliant; but assuming it to be written in earnest, we can heartily praise the form of its construction without agreeing with the sentiments expressed.'—*St. James's Gazette.*

Shows considerable power and aptitude.'—*Saturday Review.*

'The book is extremely clever and some of the situations very striking, while there are sketches of character which really live. The final *dénouement* might at first sight be thought impossible, but the effect on those who take part in it is so free of exaggeration, that we can almost imagine that such people are in our midst.'—*Guardian.*

POOR FOLK. Translated from the Russian of FEDOR DOSTOIEVSKY. By LENA MILMAN. With an Introduction by GEORGE MOORE, and a Title-page and Cover Design by AUBREY BEARDSLEY. Crown 8vo, 3s. 6d. net.

'The book is cleverly translated. "Poor Folk" gains in reality and pathos by the very means that in less skilful hands would be tedious and commonplace.'—*Spectator.*

'A charming story of the love of a Charles Lamb kind of old bachelor for a young work-girl. Full of quiet humour and still more full of the *lachrymæ rerum.*'—*Star.*

'Scenes of poignant realism, described with so admirable a blending of humour and pathos that they haunt the memory.'—*Daily News.*

'No one will read it attentively without feeling both its power and its pathos.'—*Scotsman.*

'The book is one of great pathos and absorbing interest. Miss Milman has given us an admirable version of it which will commend itself to every one who cares for good literature.'—*Glasgow Herald.*

'These things seem small, but in the hands of Dostoievsky they make a work of genius.'—*Black and White.*

'One of the most pathetic things in all literature, heartrending just because its tragedy is so repressed.'—*Bookman.*

'As to novels, the very finest I have read of late or for long is "Poor Folk, by Fedor Dostoievsky, translated by Miss Lena Milman."'—*Truth.*

'A book to be read for the merits of its execution. The translator by the way has turned it into excellent English.'—*Pall Mall Gazette.*

'The narrative vibrates with feeling, and these few unstudied letters convey to us a cry from the depths of a famished human soul. As far as we can judge, the English rendering, though simple, retains that ring of emotion which must distinguish the original.'—*Westminster Review.*

'One of the most striking studies in plain and simple realism which was ever written.'—*Daily Telegraph.*

'"Poor Folk" is certainly a vivid and pathetic story.'—*Globe.*

'A triumph of realistic art—a masterpiece of a great writer.'—*Morning Post.*

'Dostoievsky's novel has met with that rare advantage, a really good translator.'—*Queen.*

'This admirable translation of a great author.'—*Liverpool Mercury.*

'"Poor Folk" Englished does not read like a translation—indubitably a masterpiece.'—*Literary World.*

'Told with a gradually deepening intensity and force, a pathetic truthfulness which lives in the memory.'—*Leeds Mercury.*

'What Charles Dickens in his attempts to reproduce the sentiment and pathos of the humble deceived himself and others into thinking that he did, that Fedor Dostoievsky actually does.'—*Manchester Guardian.*

'It is a story that leaves the reader almost stunned. Miss Milman's translation is admirable.'—*Gentlewoman.*

'The translation appears to be well done so far as we have compared it with the original.'—W. R. MORFILL in *The Academy.*

'A most impressive and characteristic specimen of Russian fiction. Those to whom Russian is a sealed book will be duly grateful to the translator (who has acquitted herself excellently), to Mr. Moore, and to the publisher for this presentment of Dostoievsky's remarkable novel.'—*Times.*

A CHILD OF THE AGE. By FRANCIS ADAMS. Title-page and Cover Design by AUBREY BEARDSLEY. Crown 8vo, 3s. 6d. net.

'English or foreign, there is no work among those now before me which is so original as that of the late Francis Adams. "A Child of the Age" is original, moving, often fascinating.'—*Academy.*

'A great deal of cleverness and perhaps something more has gone to the writing of "A Child of the Age."'—*Vanity Fair.*

'It comes recognisably near to great excellence. There is a love episode in this book which is certainly fine. Clearly conceived and expressed with point.'—*Pall Mall Gazette.*

'Those whose actual experience or natural intuition will enable them to see beneath the mere narrative, will appreciate the perfect art with which a boy of nineteen—this was the author's age when the book was written—has treated one of the most delicate subjects on which a man can write—the history of his own innermost feelings.'—*Weekly Sun.*

'The book possesses a depth and clearness of insight, a delicacy of touch, and a brilliancy and beauty of style very remarkable in so young a writer.' —*Weekly Scotsman.*

'"A Child of the Age" is as fully saturated with the individuality of its author as "Wuthering Heights" was saturated with the individuality of Emily Brontë.'—*Daily Chronicle.*

'I am writing about the book because it is one you should read, for it is typical of a certain sort of character and contains some indubitable excellences.'—*Pall Mall Budget.*

'Not faultless, indeed, but touched with the magic of real poetry; without the elaborate carving of the chisel. The love incident is exquisite and exquisitely told. "Rosy" lives; her emotions stir us. Wonderfully suggested in several parts of the work is the severe irony of nature before profound human suffering.'—*Saturday Review.*

'There is a bloom of romance upon their story which recalls Lucy and Richard Feverel. . . . . It is rarely that a novelist is able to suffuse his story with the first rosy purity of passion as Mr. Adams has done in this book.'—*Realm.*

'Only a man of big talent could have produced it.'—*Literary World.*

'A tale of fresh originality, deep spiritual meaning, and exceptional power. It fairly buds, blossoms, and fruits with suggestions that search the human spirit through. No similar production has come from the hand of any author in our time. It exalts, inspires, comforts, and strengthens all together. It instructs by suggestion, spiritualises the thought by its elevating and purifying narrative, and feeds the hungering spirit with food it is only too ready to accept and assimilate.'—*Boston Courier, U.S.A.*

'It is a remarkable work—as a pathological study almost unsurpassed. It produces the impression of a photograph from life, so vividly realistic is the treatment. To this result the author's style, with its fidelity of microscopic detail, doubtless contributes.'—*Evening Traveller, U.S.A.*

'The story by Francis Adams is one to read slowly, and then to read a second time. It is powerfully written, full of strong suggestion, unlike, in fact, anything we have recently read. What he would have done in the way of literary creation, had he lived, is, of course, only a matter of conjecture. What he did we have before us in this remarkable book.'—*Boston Advertiser, U.S.A.*

Second Edition now ready.

THE GREAT GOD PAN AND THE INMOST LIGHT.
By ARTHUR MACHEN. With Title-page and Cover Design by AUBREY BEARDSLEY. Crown 8vo, 3s. 6d. net.

'Since Mr. Stevenson played with the crucibles of science in "Dr. Jekyll and Mr. Hyde" we have not encountered a more successful experiment of the sort.'—*Pall Mall Gazette.*

'Nothing so appalling as these tales has been given to publicity within our remembrance; in which, nevertheless, such ghastly fictions as Poe's "Telltale Heart," Bulwer's "The House and the Brain," and Le Fanu's "In a Glass Darkly" still are vividly present. The supernatural element is utilised with extraordinary power and effectiveness in both these blood-chilling masterpieces.'—*Daily Telegraph.*

'He imparts the shudder of awe without giving rise to a feeling of disgust. Let me strongly advise anyone anxious for a real, durable thrill, to get it.'—*Woman.*

'A nightmarish business it is—suggested, seemingly, by "Dr. Jekyll and Mr. Hyde"—and capital reading, we should say, for ghouls and vampires in their leisure moments.'—*Daily Chronicle.*

'The rest we leave for those whose nerves are strong, merely saying that since "Dr. Jekyll and Mr. Hyde," we have read nothing so uncanny.'—*The Literary World.*

'The literature of the "supernatural" has recently been supplemented by two striking books, which carry on with much ability the traditions of Sheridan Le Fanu: one is "The Great God Pan," by Arthur Machen.'—*Star.*

'Will arouse the sort of interest that was created by "Dr. Jekyll and Mr. Hyde." The tales present a frankly impossible horror, which, nevertheless, kindles the imagination and excites a powerful curiosity. It is almost a book of genius, and we are not sure that the safeguarding adverb is not superfluous.'—*Birmingham Post.*

'The coarser terrors of Edgar Allen Poe do not leave behind them the shudder that one feels at the shadowed devil-mysteries of "The Great God Pan."'—*Liverpool Mercury.*

'If any one labours under a burning desire to experience the sensation familiarly known as making one's flesh creep, he can hardly do better than read "The Great God Pan."'—*Speaker.*

'For sheer gruesome horror Mr. Machen's story, "The Great God Pan," surpasses anything that has been published for a long time.'—*Scotsman.*

'Nothing more striking or more skilful than this book has been produced in the way of what one may call Borderland fiction since Mr. Stevenson's indefatigable Brownies gave the world "Dr. Jekyll and Mr. Hyde."'—*Glasgow Herald.*

'The mysteries he deals with lie far beyond the reach of ordinary human experience, and as they are vague, though so horror-producing, he wisely treats them with a reticence that, while it accords with the theme, immensely heightens the effect.'—*Dundee Advertiser.*

'The author is an artist, and tells his tale with reticence and grace, hinting the demoniac secret at first obscurely, and only gradually permitting the reader to divine how near to us are the infernal powers, and how terribly they satiate their lusts and wreak their malice upon mankind. It is a work of something like genius, fascinating and fearsome.'—*Bradford Observer.*

'They are fitting companions to the famous stories by Edgar Allan Poe both in matter and style,'—*Boston Home Journal, U.S.A.*

'They are horror stories, the horror being of the vague psychologic kind and dependent in each case upon a man of science, who tries to effect a change in individual personality by an operation upon the brain cells. The implied lesson is that it is dangerous and unwise to seek to probe the mystery separating mind and matter. These sketches are extremely strong, and we guarantee the shivers to any one who reads them.'—*Hartford Courant, U.S.A.*

Fourth Edition now ready.

DISCORDS. By GEORGE EGERTON. With Title-page and Cover Design by AUBREY BEARDSLEY. Crown 8vo, 3s. 6d. net.

'We have the heights as well as the depths of life. The transforming touch of beauty is upon it, of that poetry of conception beneath whose spell nothing is ugly or unclean.'—*Star.*

'The writer is a warm-blooded enthusiast, not a cold-blooded "scientist." In the long run perhaps it will do some good.'—*National Observer.*

'The power and passion which every reader felt in "Keynotes" are equally present in this new volume. But there is also in at least equal measure that artistic force and skill which went so far to overcome the repugnance which many felt to the painful dissection of feminine nature.'—*North British Daily Mail.*

'Force of conception and power of vivid presentment mark these sketches, and are sure to impress all who read them.'—*Birmingham Post.*

'Written with all "George Egerton's" eloquence and fervour.'—*Yorkshire Herald.*

'It almost takes one's breath away by its prodigious wrong-headedness, its sheer impudence.'—MR. A. B. WALKLEY in *The Morning Leader.*

'The wonderful power of observation, the close analysis and the really brilliant writing revealed in parts of this volume.... "George Egerton" would seem to be well equipped for the task.'—*Cork Examiner.*

'Readers who have a leaning to psychological fiction, and who revel in such studies of character as George Meredith's "Diana of the Crossways" will find much to interest them in these clever stories.'—*Western Daily Press.*

'There is no escape from the fact that it is vividly interesting.'—*The Christian World.*

'With all her realism there is a refinement and a pathos and a brilliance of style that lift the book into a region altogether removed from the merely sensational or the merely repulsive. It is a book that one might read with a pencil in his hand, for it is studded with many fine, vivid passages.'—*Weekly Scotsman.*

'She has many fine qualities. Her work throbs with temperament, and here and there we come upon touches that linger in the memory as of things felt and seen, not read of.'—*Daily News.*

'Mrs. Grundy, to whom they would be salutary, will not be induced to read either "Keynotes" or "Discords."'—*Westminster Gazette.*

'What an absorbing, wonderful book it is: How absolutely sincere, and how finely wrong! George Egerton may be what the indefatigable Mr. Zangwill calls a one-I'd person, but she is a literary artist of exceptional endowment—probably a genius.'—*Woman.*

'She has given, times without number, examples of her ripening powers that astonish us. Her themes astound; her audacity is tremendous. In the many great passages an advance is proved that is little short of amazing.'—*Literary World.*

'Interesting and skilfully written.'—*Sunday Times.*

'A series of undoubtedly clever stories, told with a poetic dreaminess which softens the rugged truths of which they treat. Mothers might benefit themselves and convey help to young girls who are about to be married by the perusal of its pages.'—*Liverpool Mercury.*

'They are the work of an author of considerable power, not to say genius. —*Scotsman.*

'The book is true to human nature, for the author has genius, and, let us add, has heart. It is representative; it is, in the hackneyed phrase, a human document.'—*Speaker.*

'It is another note in the great chorus of revolt . . . on the whole clearer, more eloquent, and braver than almost any I have yet heard.'— T. P. ('Book of the Week'), *Weekly Sun,* December 30.

'These masterly word-sketches.'—*Daily Telegraph.*

'Were it possible to have my favourite sketches and stories from both volumes ("Keynotes" and "Discords") bound together in one, I should look upon myself as a very fortunate traveller; one who had great pleasure, if not exactly happiness, within her reach.'—*Lady's Pictorial.*

'But in all this there is a rugged grandeur of style, a keen analysis of motive, and a deepness of pathos that stamp George Egerton as one of the greatest women writers of the day.'—*Boston Traveller, U.S.A.*

'The story of the child, of the girl, and of the woman is told, and told by one to whom the mysteries of the life of each are familiarly known, In their very truth, as the writer has so subtly analysed her triple characters, they sadden one to think that such things must be; yet as they are real, they are bound to be disclosed by somebody, and in due time.'—*Boston Courier, U.S.A.*

Sixteenth Edition just ready.

THE WOMAN WHO DID. By GRANT ALLEN. With Title-page and Cover Design by AUBREY BEARDSLEY. Crown 8vo, 3s. 6d. net.

'There is not a sensual thought or suggestion throughout the whole volume. Though I dislike and disbelieve in his gospel, I thoroughly respect Mr. Grant Allen for having stated it so honourably and so bravely.' —*Academy.*

'Even its bitterest enemies must surely feel some thrill of admiration for its courage. It is, once more, one philosopher against the world. Not in our day, perhaps, can it be decided which is right, Mr. Grant Allen, or the world. Perhaps our children's children will some day be canonising Mr. Grant Allen for the very book for which to-day he stands a much greater chance of being stoned, and happy lovers of the new era bless the name of the man who, almost single-handed, fought the battle of Free Love. Time alone can say. . . . None but the most foolish or malignant reader of 'The Woman Who Did' can fail to recognise the noble purpose which animates its pages. . . . Label it as one will, it remains a clever, stimulating book. A real enthusiasm for humanity blazes through every page of this, in many ways, remarkable and significant little book.'—*Sketch.*

'The book is interesting, as embodying the carefully thought-out theories of so distinguished a writer.'—*Literary World.*

'Mr. Grant Allen has undoubtedly produced an epoch-making book, and one which will be a living voice when most of the novels of this generation have passed away into silence. It is epoch-making in the sense that "Uncle Tom's Cabin" was;—the literary merits of that work were by no means great, but yet it rang like a tocsin through the land, arousing mankind to a sense of the slavery under which a large portion of humanity suffered.'—*Humanitarian.*

'Interesting, and even absorbing.'—*Weekly Sun.*

'His sincerity is undeniable. And in the mouth of Herminia are some very noble and eloquent passages upon the wrongs of our marriage system.'—*Pall Mall Gazette.*

'A tale of purity and innocence unparalleled since the "Garden of Eden" or "Paul and Virginia."'—*Daily Express.*

'A remarkable and powerful story. It increases our respect for Mr. Allen's ability, nor do we feel inclined to join in throwing stones at him as a perverter of our morals and our social institutions. However widely we may differ from Mr. Allen's views on many important questions, we are bound to recognise his sincerity, and to respect him accordingly.'—*Speaker.*

'The story is as remarkable for its art as its daring, and well deserves a place in the remarkable series in which it has been published.'—*The Scotsman.*

'Herminia is a rare and fine creature.'—*Daily Chronicle.*

'An artist in words and a writer of deep feeling has lavished his best powers in the production of "The Woman Who Did." The story is charmingly told. Delineated with a delicacy and strength of touch that cannot but delight the most fastidious reader. Mr. Grant Allen draws a picture of a sweet and pure and beautiful woman. The book is very beautiful and very sad.'—*Liverpool Mercury.*

'The book (for it is well written and clever) ought to be the last note in the chorus of revolt. For it proves to demonstration the futility of the attempt.'—*Sun.*

'We cannot too highly commend the conspicuous and transparent purity of the handling.'—*Public Opinion.*

'He conclusively shows that if the marriage laws need revision, yet the sweetness and seemliness of home, the dignity of woman as mother or as man's helpmeet, are rooted in the sanctity of wedlock.'—*Daily News.*

'Mr. Grant Allen deserves thanks for treating with such delicacy problem which stands in such pressing need of solution as the reform of our stern marriage laws.'—*Echo.*

'Its merits are large and its interest profound.'—*Weekly Scotsman.*

'It may not merit praise, but it merits reading.'—*Saturday Review.*

PRINCE ZALESKI. By M. P. SHIEL. With Title-page by AUBREY BEARDSLEY. Crown 8vo, 3s. 6d. net.

'Mr. M. P. Shiel has in this volume produced something which is always rare, and which is every year becoming a greater rarity—a work of literary invention characterised by substantial novelty. We have Poe's analysis and Poe's glamour, but they are no longer distinct; they are combined in a new synthesis which stamps a new imaginative impression. A finely wrought structure in which no single line impairs the symmetry and proportion. One of the most boldly-planned and strikingly-executed stories of its kind which has appeared for many a long day. We believe there is nothing in "Prince Zaleski" which that great inventor and masterly manipulator of the spoils of invention (Poe) would have disdained to father.'—*Daily Chronicle.*

'Should obtain popularity. Written in an easy and clear style. The author shows an amount of ingenuity and capacity for plot considerably above the average. The reader will find it difficult to put the book down before he has satisfied his curiosity to the last page.'—*Weekly Sun.*

'The Prince was a Sherlock Holmes, with this difference: that while yielding nothing to Conan Doyle's hero in mere intellectual agility, he had that imaginative insight which makes poets more frequently than detectives. Sherlock Holmes was a clever but essentially commonplace man. Prince Zaleski was a great man, simply. Enthralling . . . once begun they insist on being finished. Broadly and philosophically conceived, and put together with rare narrative skill, and feeling for effect.'—*Woman.*

There is a strange, fantastic ingenuity in all the stories, while a strong dash of mysticism gives them a peculiar flavour that differentiates them from the ordinary detective story. They are clever and curious, and will appeal to all lovers of the transcendental and improbable.'—*The Scotsman.*

'Thoroughly entertaining, and the chief figure is undeniably picturesque.'—*Yorkshire Post.*

'An abundance of ingenuity and quaint out-of-the-way learning mark the three stories contained in this volume.'—*Liverpool Mercury.*

'He has imparted to the three tales in this volume something of that atmosphere of eerie fantasy which Poe knew how to conjure, proceeding by the analysis of a baffling intricacy of detail to an unforeseen conclusion. The themes and their treatment are alike highly imaginative.'—*Daily News.*

'Manifestly written by one of Poe's true disciples. His analytical skill is not that of the detective, even of so brilliant a detective as Mr. Sherlock Holmes. Probably his exploits will interest the public far less than did those of Mr. Doyle's famous character; but the select few, who can appreciate delicate work, will delight in them exceedingly.'—*Speaker.*

'Truth to tell we like our Sherlock better in his new dress. The book will please those who love a good old-fashioned riddle, and a good new-fangled answer.'—*National Observer.*

'Has genuine literary merit, and possesses entrancing interest. A kind of Sherlock Holmes, though of a far more finished type than Mr. Conan Doyle's famous creation. The remarkable ingenuity of Mr. Shiel—worthy of Edgar Allen Poe at his best—in tracing out the mystery surrounding the death of Lord Pharanx, the Stone of the Edmundsbury Monks, and the Society of Sparta, constitutes a veritable *tour de force*. We have nothing but praise for this extraordinarily clever and interesting volume.'—*Whitehall Review.*

'Worked out very ingeniously, and we are thoroughly impressed by the Prince's mental powers.'—*Sunday Times.*

'A clever, extravagant, and lurid little book.'—*Westminster Gazette.*

'Mr. Shiel's mysteries are very good, and he has put them into literary form.'—*Bookman.*

'They are fascinating in spite of the demands they make upon our credulity.'—*Times.*

'Imagination of the weirdest and the strangest runs rife. The personage of the title is a sort of *dilettante* Sherlock Holmes, but with far weirder problems to unravel than ever fell to the lot of Dr. Doyle's detective. The book contains three stories, reminding one now of Poe and now of Stevenson's "New Arabian Nights," all told with convincing art and a power of uncommon invention which few writers have equalled. Will give you some exciting hours.'—*Review of Reviews.*

WOMEN'S TRAGEDIES. By H. D. LOWRY. With Title-page and Cover Design by AUBREY BEARDSLEY. Crown 8vo, 3s. 6d. net.

'He is the master of a style singularly strenuous and sensitive. What he sees he can express with marvellous vividness. There is nothing more terrible and perfect of its kind than his story, "The Man in the Room." It is magnificently done, powerfully imagined, and convincingly presented.'—*Black and White.*

'Mr. Lowry's "Women's Tragedies" are the most striking thumbnail sketches since Mr. Quiller Couch idly ceased to write his wonderful "Noughts and Crosses."'—*Star.*

'A collection of vivid sketches from life.'—*Liverpool Mercury.*

'A wide and critical section of the reading public will be ready to welcome "Women's Tragedies." The author has not a little of the ancient mariner's power. He creates a situation which holds the reader mentally spellbound, and leaves an impression not readily effaced ... sombre, even eerie, they prove, and yet strong with the author's power to fascinate.'—*Dundee Advertiser.*

'The chief charm of the stories is the delicacy and strength with which they are wrought, and the genuine insight into human nature which they show.'—*Scotsman.*

'He is a master of a simple, forcible style; he has a deep insight into human nature, a strong and active imagination; and, above all, he has that indescribable knack of making interesting the commonplace things of existence. This collection of stories will be read with genuine pleasure, and will do much to advance the reputation of the author.'—*Weekly Scotsman.*

'In Mr. Lowry's latest book we have some healthy studies of human nature, stories which are full of strong, deep, and simple emotion. This is the fiction, simple and human, real and beautiful, which rebukes at one and the same time the sentimentality of English art and the unhealthiness of French.'—*Western Daily Mercury.*

'It is a profoundly interesting and powerful volume.'—*Whitehall Review.*

'"The Man in the Room" is certainly the strongest. There is a subtle and complete knowledge of the woman of the tragedy, an insight and mastery which is never paraded, but is governed, restrained, and used. The author is an artist well understanding the use of a touch of the grotesque for the heightening of the tragedy.'—*Realm.*

'His stories are clever and intensely dramatic. We cannot overlook the power of imagination and of literary expression which Mr. Lowry's book reveals. Stamps its writer as a man of great gifts.'—*Independent.*

'Is written with a good deal of distinction. No one can deny the charm of such stories as "Beauty's Lovers" and "The Sisters," and "The Man in the Room" has both a gracefully drawn heroine and a good deal of weird power.'—*Queen.*

'He can imagine scenes and incidents of the most dramatic intensity and put them before us in half a dozen pages.'—*Glasgow Evening News.*

'Remind us frequently of Mr. Hardy's "Life's Little Ironies." Exhibit no little artistic power.'—*Methodist Recorder.*

'Are very real and strong, very grim. The language is very simple, direct, and, in necessary consequence, expressive.'—*National Observer.*

'The stories are told in fresh, bright, unaffected fashion.'—*Sunday Times.*

AT THE FIRST CORNER, AND OTHER STORIES. By H. B. MARRIOTT WATSON. With Title-page and Cover Design by AUBREY BEARDSLEY. Crown 8vo, 3s. 6d. net.

'We willingly bear witness to Mr. Watson's brilliance, versatility, and literary power. "An Ordeal of Three" is a fancy that is full of beauty and delicate charm. When, again, Mr. Watson deals with the merely sordid and real side of East-end London he justifies his choice by a certain convincing realism which is never dull, and which is always inevitably true.'—*Pall Mall Gazette.*

'Made up of exceedingly good stories. . . . The mere writing of them makes them a pleasure to read.'—*Star.*

'Have the charm of individuality.'—*Globe.*

'Exceedingly well written. There is no denying Mr. Marriott Watson's strength and delicacy of style.'—*Queen.*

'There is an impressive "grip" in Mr. Watson's narrative from which the reader cannot easily escape.'—*Whitehall Review.*

'They all show a vigorous pen and a command of forcible language.'—*Dundee Advertiser.*

'The stories are all told with very considerable vigour and skill, and show a strong vein of imagination.'—*Scotsman.*

'Mr. Marriott Watson can write, and in these new stories he shows, more manifestly than in any previous work, his capacity for dramatic realisation. "An Ordeal of Three" has not only strength but charm.'—*Daily Chronicle.*

'Admirably conceived and brilliantly finished; the book will be read.'—*Saturday Review.*

'Knowledge of life, literary cleverness, charm, and, above all, style, are present all through. One cannot dip into his volume without being taken captive and reading every story.'—*Realm.*

'Remarkable for diversity of subject and distinction of style. Every page of this charming volume is original.'—*Black and White.*

'Mr. Watson can tell a story in a terse, vigorous, and thrilling manner.'—*Westminster Gazette.*

'Contains the best work he has yet done. Uncommonly well written.'—*Sketch.*

'There is undeniable power in the volume of stories, "At the First Corner," and there is something very like the fire of genius behind this power. The style is terse, vivid, and imaginative.'—*Guardian.*

List of Books in Belles Lettres

ALL BOOKS IN THIS CATALOGUE
ARE PUBLISHED AT NET PRICES

1895

Telegraphic Address—
'BODLEIAN, LONDON'

1895.

List of Books
IN
BELLES LETTRES
(*Including some Transfers*)

Published by John Lane
The Bodley Head
VIGO STREET, LONDON, W.

N.B.—The Authors and Publisher reserve the right of reprinting any book in this list if a new edition is called for, except in cases where a stipulation has been made to the contrary, and of printing a separate edition of any of the books for America irrespective of the numbers to which the English editions are limited. The numbers mentioned do not include copies sent to the public libraries, nor those sent for review.

Most of the books are published simultaneously in England and America, and in many instances the names of the American Publishers are appended.

ADAMS (FRANCIS).
    ESSAYS IN MODERNITY. Crown 8vo. 5s. net. [*Shortly.*
    Chicago: Stone & Kimball.

    A CHILD OF THE AGE. (*See* KEYNOTES SERIES.)

ALLEN (GRANT).
    THE LOWER SLOPES: A Volume of Verse. With Title-page and Cover Design by J. ILLINGWORTH KAY. 600 copies. Crown 8vo. 5s. net.
    Chicago: Stone & Kimball.
    THE WOMAN WHO DID. (*See* KEYNOTES SERIES.)

BEARDSLEY (AUBREY).
    The Story of Venus and Tannhäuser, in which is set forth an exact account of the Manner of State held by Madam Venus, Goddess and Meretrix, under the famous Hörselberg, and containing the adventures of Tannhäuser in that place, his repentance, his journeying to Rome, and return to the loving mountain. By Aubrey Beardsley. With 20 full-page illustrations, numerous ornaments, and a cover from the same hand. Sq. 16mo. 10s. 6d. net. [*In preparation.*

BEDDOES (T. L.).
    See Gosse (Edmund).

BEECHING (Rev. H. C.).
    In a Garden: Poems. With Title-page designed by Roger Fry. Crown 8vo. 5s. net.
    New York: Macmillan & Co.

BENSON (ARTHUR CHRISTOPHER).
    Lyrics. Fcap. 8vo., buckram. 5s. net.
    New York: Macmillan & Co.

BROTHERTON (MARY).
    Rosemary for Remembrance. With Title-page and Cover Design by Walter West. Fcap. 8vo. 3s. 6d. net.

CAMPBELL (GERALD).
    The Joneses and the Asterisks. With 6 Illustrations and a Title-page by F. H. Townsend. Fcap. 8vo. 3s. 6d. net.
    New York: The Merriam Co.

CASTLE (Mrs. EGERTON).
    My Little Lady Anne: A Romance. Sq. 16mo. 2s. 6d. net. [*In preparation.*
    Philadelphia: Henry Altemus.

CASTLE (EGERTON).
    See Stevenson (Robert Louis).

CROSS (VICTORIA).
    Consummation: A Novel. Crown 8vo. 4s. 6d. net.
    [*In preparation.*

DALMON (C. W.).
    Song Favours. With a specially-designed Title-page. Sq. 16mo. 4s. 6d. net. [*In preparation.*
    Chicago: Way & Williams.

D'ARCY (ELLA).
  MONOCHROMES. (*See* KEYNOTES SERIES.)

DAVIDSON (JOHN).
  PLAYS: An Unhistorical Pastoral; A Romantic Farce; Bruce, a Chronicle Play; Smith, a Tragic Farce; Scaramouch in Naxos, a Pantomime, with a Frontispiece and Cover Design by AUBREY BEARDSLEY. Printed at the Ballantyne Press. 500 copies. Small 4to. 7s. 6d. net.
    Chicago: Stone & Kimball.
  FLEET STREET ECLOGUES. Fcap. 8vo, buckram. 5s. net. [*Out of Print at present.*
  A RANDOM ITINERARY AND A BALLAD. With a Frontispiece and Title-page by LAURENCE HOUSMAN. 600 copies. Fcap. 8vo, Irish Linen. 5s. net.
    Boston: Copeland & Day.
  BALLADS AND SONGS. With a Title-page and Cover Design by WALTER WEST. Third Edition. Fcap. 8vo, buckram. 5s. net.
    Boston: Copeland & Day.

DAWE (W. CARLTON).
  YELLOW AND WHITE. (*See* KEYNOTES SERIES.)

DE TABLEY (LORD).
  POEMS, DRAMATIC AND LYRICAL. By JOHN LEICESTER WARREN (Lord De Tabley). Illustrations and Cover Design by C. S. RICKETTS. Second Edition. Crown 8vo. 7s. 6d. net.
    New York: Macmillan & Co.
  POEMS, DRAMATIC AND LYRICAL. Second Series, uniform in binding with the former volume. Crown 8vo. 5s. net.
    New York: Macmillan & Co.

DIX (GERTRUDE).
  THE GIRL FROM THE FARM. (*See* KEYNOTES SERIES.)

DOSTOIEVSKY (F.).
  See KEYNOTES SERIES, Vol. III.

ECHEGARAY (JOSÉ).
See LYNCH (HANNAH).

EGERTON (GEORGE).
KEYNOTES. (*See* KEYNOTES SERIES.)
DISCORDS. (*See* KEYNOTES SERIES.)
YOUNG OFEG'S DITTIES. A translation from the Swedish of OLA HANSSON. Crown 8vo. 3s. 6d. net.
Boston: Roberts Bros.

FARR (FLORENCE).
THE DANCING FAUN. (*See* KEYNOTES SERIES.)

FLETCHER (J. S.).
THE WONDERFUL WAPENTAKE. By 'A SON OF THE SOIL.' With 18 full-page Illustrations by J. A. SYMINGTON. Crown 8vo. 5s. 6d. net.
Chicago: A. C. M'Clurg & Co.

GALE (NORMAN).
ORCHARD SONGS. With Title-page and Cover Design by J. ILLINGWORTH KAY. Fcap. 8vo, Irish Linen. 5s. net.
Also a Special Edition limited in number on hand-made paper bound in English vellum. £1, 1s. net.
New York: G. P. Putnam's Sons.

GARNETT (RICHARD).
POEMS. With Title-page by J. ILLINGWORTH KAY. 350 copies. Crown 8vo. 5s. net.
Boston: Copeland & Day.
DANTE, PETRARCH, CAMOENS, cxxlv Sonnets, rendered in English. Crown 8vo. 5s. net. [*In preparation.*

GEARY (NEVILL).
A LAWYER'S WIFE: A Novel. Crown 8vo. 4s. 6d. net. [*In preparation.*

GOSSE (EDMUND).
THE LETTERS OF THOMAS LOVELL BEDDOES. Now first edited. Pott 8vo. 5s. net.
Also 25 copies large paper. 12s. 6d. net.
New York: Macmillan & Co.

GRAHAME (KENNETH).
PAGAN PAPERS : A Volume of Essays. With Title-page by AUBREY BEARDSLEY. Fcap. 8vo. 5s. net.
Chicago : Stone & Kimball.

THE GOLDEN AGE. Crown 8vo. 3s. 6d. net.
Chicago : Stone & Kimball.

GREENE (G. A.).
ITALIAN LYRISTS OF TO-DAY. Translations in the original metres from about thirty-five living Italian poets, with bibliographical and biographical notes. Crown 8vo. 5s. net.
New York : Macmillan & Co.

GREENWOOD (FREDERICK).
IMAGINATION IN DREAMS. Crown 8vo. 5s. net.
New York : Macmillan & Co.

HAKE (T. GORDON).
A SELECTION FROM HIS POEMS. Edited by Mrs. MEYNELL. With a Portrait after D. G. ROSSETTI, and a Cover Design by GLEESON WHITE. Crown 8vo. 5s. net.
Chicago : Stone & Kimball.

HANSSON (LAURA MARHOLM).
MODERN WOMEN : Six Psychological Sketches. [Sophia Kovalevsky, George Egerton, Eleanora Duse, Amalie Skram, Marie Bashkirtseff, A. Edgren Leffler]. Translated from the German by HERMIONE RAMSDEN. Crown 8vo. 3s. 6d. net. [*In preparation.*

HANSSON (OLA). See EGERTON.

HARLAND (HENRY).
GREY ROSES. (*See* KEYNOTES SERIES.)

HAYES (ALFRED).
THE VALE OF ARDEN AND OTHER POEMS. With a Title-page and a Cover designed by E. H. NEW. Fcap. 8vo. 3s. 6d. net.
Also 25 copies large paper. 15s. net.

HEINEMANN (WILLIAM)
THE FIRST STEP ; A Dramatic Moment. Small 4to. 3s. 6d. net.

HOPPER (NORA).
   BALLADS IN PROSE. With a Title-page and Cover by WALTER WEST. Sq. 16mo. 5s. net.
   Boston: Roberts Bros.

HOUSMAN (LAURENCE).
   GREEN ARRAS: Poems. With Illustrations by the Author. Crown 8vo. 5s. net. [*In preparation.*

IRVING (LAURENCE).
   GODEFROI AND YOLANDE: A Play. With three Illustrations by AUBREY BEARDSLEY. Sm. 4to. 5s. net.
                                                  [*In preparation.*

JAMES (W. P.).
   ROMANTIC PROFESSIONS: A Volume of Essays. With Title-page designed by J. ILLINGWORTH KAY. Crown 8vo. 5s. net.
   New York: Macmillan & Co.

JOHNSON (LIONEL).
   THE ART OF THOMAS HARDY: Six Essays. With Etched Portrait by WM. STRANG, and Bibliography by JOHN LANE. Second Edition. Crown 8vo. 5s. 6d. net.
     Also 150 copies, large paper, with proofs of the portrait. £1, 1s. net.
   New York: Dodd, Mead & Co.

JOHNSON (PAULINE).
   WHITE WAMPUM: Poems. With a Title-page and Cover Design by E. H. NEW. Crown 8vo. 5s. net.
   Boston: Lamson Wolffe & Co.

JOHNSTONE (C. E.).
   BALLADS OF BOY AND BEAK. With a Title-page by F. H. TOWNSEND. Sq. 32mo. 2s. 6d. net. [*In preparation.*

KEYNOTES SERIES.
   Each volume with specially-designed Title-page by AUBREY BEARDSLEY. Crown 8vo, cloth. 3s. 6d. net.
   Vol. I. KEYNOTES. By GEORGE EGERTON.
                                  [*Seventh edition now ready.*
   Vol. II. THE DANCING FAUN. By FLORENCE FARR.
   Vol. III. POOR FOLK. Translated from the Russian of F. Dostoievsky by LENA MILMAN. With a Preface by GEORGE MOORE.
   Vol. IV. A CHILD OF THE AGE. By FRANCIS ADAMS.

KEYNOTES SERIES—*continued.*

    Vol. V. THE GREAT GOD PAN AND THE INMOST LIGHT. By ARTHUR MACHEN.
            [*Second edition now ready.*
    Vol. VI. DISCORDS. By GEORGE EGERTON.
            [*Fourth edition now ready.*
    Vol. VII. PRINCE ZALESKI. By M. P. SHIEL.
    Vol. VIII. THE WOMAN WHO DID. By GRANT ALLEN.
            [*Seventeenth edition now ready.*
    Vol. IX. WOMEN'S TRAGEDIES. By H. D. LOWRY.
    Vol. X. GREY ROSES. By HENRY HARLAND.
    Vol. XI. AT THE FIRST CORNER AND OTHER STORIES. By H. B. MARRIOTT WATSON.
    Vol. XII. MONOCHROMES. By ELLA D'ARCY.
    Vol. XIII. AT THE RELTON ARMS. By EVELYN SHARP.
    Vol. XIV. THE GIRL FROM THE FARM. By GERTRUDE DIX.
    Vol. XV. THE MIRROR OF MUSIC. By STANLEY V. MAKOWER.
    Vol. XVI. YELLOW AND WHITE. By W. CARLTON DAWE.
    Vol. XVII. THE MOUNTAIN LOVERS. By FIONA MACLEOD.
    Vol. XVIII. THE THREE IMPOSTORS. By ARTHUR MACHEN.
        Boston: Roberts Bros.

LANDER (HARRY).
    WEIGHED IN THE BALANCE: A Novel. Crown 8vo. 4s. 6d. net. [*In preparation.*

LANG (ANDREW).
    See STODDART.

LEATHER (R. K.).
    VERSES. 250 copies. Fcap. 8vo. 3s. net.
      Transferred by the Author to the present Publisher.

LE GALLIENNE (RICHARD).
    PROSE FANCIES. With Portrait of the Author by WILSON STEER. Fourth Edition. Crown 8vo. Purple cloth. 5s. net.
      Also a limited large paper edition. 12s. 6d. net.
      New York: G. P. Putnam's Sons.

LE GALLIENNE (RICHARD).
THE BOOK BILLS OF NARCISSUS, An Account rendered by RICHARD LE GALLIENNE. Third Edition. With a Frontispiece. Crown 8vo. Purple cloth. 3s. 6d. net.
Also 50 copies on large paper. 8vo. 10s. 6d. net.
New York: G. P. Putnam's Sons.
ROBERT LOUIS STEVENSON, AN ELEGY, AND OTHER POEMS, MAINLY PERSONAL. With Etched Title-page by D. Y. CAMERON. Cr. 8vo. Purple cloth. 4s. 6d. net.
Also 75 copies on large paper. 8vo. 12s. 6d. net.
Boston: Copeland & Day.
ENGLISH POEMS. Fourth Edition, revised. Crown 8vo. Purple cloth. 4s. 6d. net.
Boston: Copeland & Day.
RETROSPECTIVE REVIEWS, A LITERARY LOG, 1891-1895. 2 vols. Crown 8vo. Purple cloth. 7s. net.
New York: Dodd, Mead & Co. [*In preparation.*
GEORGE MEREDITH: Some Characteristics. With a Bibliography (much enlarged) by JOHN LANE, portrait, etc. Fourth Edition. Cr. 8vo. Purple cloth. 5s. 6d. net.
THE RELIGION OF A LITERARY MAN. 5th thousand. Crown 8vo. Purple cloth. 3s. 6d. net.
Also a special rubricated edition on hand-made paper. 8vo. 10s. 6d. net.
New York: G. P. Putnam's Sons.

LOWRY (H. D.).
WOMEN'S TRAGEDIES. (*See* KEYNOTES SERIES.)

LUCAS (WINIFRED).
A VOLUME OF POEMS. Fcap. 8vo. 4s. 6d. net.
[*In preparation.*

LYNCH (HANNAH).
THE GREAT GALEOTO AND FOLLY OR SAINTLINESS. Two Plays, from the Spanish of JOSÉ ECHEGARAY, with an Introduction. Small 4to. 5s. 6d. net.
Boston: Lamson Wolffe & Co.

MACHEN (ARTHUR).
THE GREAT GOD PAN. (*See* KEYNOTES SERIES.)
THE THREE IMPOSTORS. (*See* KEYNOTES SERIES.)

MACLEOD (FIONA).
THE MOUNTAIN LOVERS. (*See* KEYNOTES SERIES.)

MAKOWER (STANLEY V.).
　THE MIRROR OF MUSIC. (*See* KEYNOTES SERIES.)

MARZIALS (THEO.).
　THE GALLERY OF PIGEONS AND OTHER POEMS. Post 8vo. 4s. 6d. net. [*Very few remain.*
　Transferred by the Author to the present Publisher.

MATHEW (FRANK).
　THE WOOD OF THE BRAMBLES: A Novel. Crown 8vo. 4s. 6d. net. [*In preparation.*

MEREDITH (GEORGE)
　THE FIRST PUBLISHED PORTRAIT OF THIS AUTHOR, engraved on the wood by W. BISCOMBE GARDNER, after the painting by G. F. WATTS. Proof copies on Japanese vellum, signed by painter and engraver. £1, 1s. net.

MEYNELL (MRS.), (ALICE C. THOMPSON).
　POEMS. Fcap. 8vo. 3s. 6d. net. [*Out of Print at present.*
　A few of the 50 large paper copies (First Edition) remain, 12s. 6d. net.
　THE RHYTHM OF LIFE AND OTHER ESSAYS. Second Edition. Fcap. 8vo. 3s. 6d. net.
　A few of the 50 large paper copies (First Edition) remain. 12s. 6d. net.
　See also HAKE.

MILLER (JOAQUIN).
　THE BUILDING OF THE CITY BEAUTIFUL. Fcap. 8vo. With a Decorated Cover. 5s. net.
　　Chicago: Stone & Kimball.

MILMAN (LENA).
　DOSTOIEVSKY'S POOR FOLK. (*See* KEYNOTES SERIES.)

MONKHOUSE (ALLAN).
　BOOKS AND PLAYS: A Volume of Essays on Meredith, Borrow, Ibsen, and others. 400 copies. Crown 8vo. 5s. net.
　　Philadelphia: J. B. Lippincott Co.

MOORE (GEORGE).
　See KEYNOTES SERIES, Vol. III.

NESBIT (E.).
　A POMANDER OF VERSE. With a Title-page and Cover designed by LAURENCE HOUSMAN. Crown 8vo. 5s. net. [*In preparation.*
　　Chicago: A. C. M'Clurg & Co.

NETTLESHIP (J. T.).
ROBERT BROWNING: Essays and Thoughts. Third Edition. With a Portrait. Crown 8vo. 5s. 6d. net.
New York: Chas. Scribner's Sons.

NOBLE (JAS. ASHCROFT).
THE SONNET IN ENGLAND AND OTHER ESSAYS. Title-page and Cover Design by AUSTIN YOUNG. 600 copies. Crown 8vo. 5s. net.
Also 50 copies large paper. 12s. 6d. net.

O'SHAUGHNESSY (ARTHUR).
HIS LIFE AND HIS WORK. With Selections from his Poems. By LOUISE CHANDLER MOULTON. Portrait and Cover Design. Fcap. 8vo. 5s. net.
Chicago: Stone & Kimball.

OXFORD CHARACTERS.
A series of lithographed portraits by WILL ROTHENSTEIN, with text by F. YORK POWELL and others. To be issued monthly in term. Each number will contain two portraits. Parts I. to VI. ready. 200 sets only, folio, wrapper, 5s. net per part; 25 special large paper sets containing proof impressions of the portraits signed by the artist, 10s. 6d. net per part.

PETERS (WM. THEODORE).
POSIES OUT OF RINGS. Sq. 16mo. 3s. 6d. net.
[*In preparation.*

PISSARRO (LUCIEN).
THE QUEEN OF THE FISHES. A Story of the Valois, adapted by MARGARET RUST, being a printed manuscript, decorated with pictures and other ornaments, cut on the wood by LUCIEN PISSARRO, and printed by him in divers colours and in gold at his press in Epping. Edition limited to 70 copies, each numbered and signed. Crown 8vo. on Japanese handmade paper, bound in vellum, £1 net.

PLARR (VICTOR).
IN THE DORIAN MOOD: Poems. Crown 8vo. 5s. net.
[*In preparation.*

RADFORD (DOLLIE).
SONGS AND OTHER VERSES. With a Title-page by PATTEN WILSON. Fcap. 8vo. 4s. 6d. net.
Philadelphia: J. B. Lippincott Co.

RAMSDEN (HERMIONE).
See HANSSON.

RICKETTS (C. S.) AND C. H. SHANNON.
HERO AND LEANDER. By CHRISTOPHER MARLOWE and GEORGE CHAPMAN. With Borders, Initials, and Illustrations designed and engraved on the wood by C. S. RICKETTS and C. H. SHANNON. Bound in English vellum and gold. 200 copies only. 35s. net.
Boston: Copeland & Day.

RHYS (ERNEST).
A LONDON ROSE AND OTHER RHYMES. With Title-page designed by SELWYN IMAGE. 350 copies. Crown 8vo. 5s. net.
New York: Dodd, Mead & Co.

ROBINSON (C. NEWTON).
THE VIOL OF LOVE. With Ornaments and Cover design by LAURENCE HOUSMAN. Crown 8vo. 5s. net.
Boston: Lamson Wolffe & Co.

ST. CYRES (LORD).
THE LITTLE FLOWERS OF ST. FRANCIS: A new rendering into English of the Fioretti di San Francesco. Crown 8vo. 5s. net. [*In preparation.*

SHARP (EVELYN).
AT THE RELTON ARMS. (*See* KEYNOTES SERIES.)

SHIEL (M. P.).
PRINCE ZALESKI. (*See* KEYNOTES SERIES.)

STACPOOLE (H. DE VERE).
DEATH, THE KNIGHT AND THE LADY. Sq. 16mo. 2s. 6d. net. [*In preparation.*
Philadelphia: Henry Altemus.

STEVENSON (ROBERT LOUIS).
PRINCE OTTO. A Rendering in French by EGERTON CASTLE. Crown 8vo. 5s. net. [*In preparation.*
Also 100 copies on large paper, uniform in size with the Edinburgh Edition of the Works.

STODDART (THOS. TOD).
THE DEATH WAKE. With an Introduction by ANDREW LANG. Fcap. 8vo. 5s. net. [*In preparation.*
Chicago: Way & Williams.

STREET (G. S.).
> THE AUTOBIOGRAPHY OF A BOY. Passages selected by his friend G. S. S. With Title-page designed by C. W. FURSE. Fcap. 8vo. 3s. 6d. net.
> *[Fourth Edition now ready.*
> New York: The Merriam Co.
> MINIATURES AND MOODS. Fcap. 8vo. 3s. net.
> *Transferred by the Author to the present Publisher.*
> New York: The Merriam Co.

SWETTENHAM (F. A.).
> MALAY SKETCHES. With a Title-page and Cover Design by PATTEN WILSON. Crown 8vo. 5s. net.
> New York: Macmillan & Co.

TABB (JOHN B.).
> . POEMS. Sq. 32mo. 4s. 6d. net.
> Boston: Copeland & Day.

TENNYSON (FREDERICK).
> POEMS OF THE DAY AND YEAR. Crown 8vo. 5s. net.
> *[In preparation.*

THIMM (C. A.).
> A COMPLETE BIBLIOGRAPHY OF THE ART OF FENCE, DUELLING, ETC. With Illustrations.
> *[In preparation.*

THOMPSON (FRANCIS).
> POEMS. With Frontispiece, Title-page, and Cover Design by LAURENCE HOUSMAN. Fourth Edition. Pott 4to. 5s. net.
> Boston: Copeland & Day.
> SISTER-SONGS: An Offering to Two Sisters. With Frontispiece, Title-page, and Cover Design by LAURENCE HOUSMAN. Pott 4to. 5s. net.
> Boston: Copeland & Day.

TYNAN HINKSON (KATHARINE).
> CUCKOO SONGS. With Title-page and Cover Design by LAURENCE HOUSMAN. Fcap. 8vo. 5s. net.
> Boston: Copeland & Day.
> MIRACLE PLAYS. *[In preparation.*

WATSON (ROSAMUND MARRIOTT).
> VESPERTILIA AND OTHER POEMS. With a Title-page designed by R. ANNING BELL. Fcap. 8vo. 4s. 6d. net. *[In preparation.*

WATSON (H. B. MARRIOTT).
> AT THE FIRST CORNER. (*See* KEYNOTES SERIES.)

WATSON (WILLIAM).
> ODES AND OTHER POEMS. Fourth Edition. Fcap. 8vo, buckram. 4s. 6d. net.
> New York: Macmillan & Co.
> THE ELOPING ANGELS: A Caprice. Second Edition. Square 16mo, buckram. 3s. 6d. net.
> New York: Macmillan & Co.
> EXCURSIONS IN CRITICISM: being some Prose Recreations of a Rhymer. Second Edition. Cr. 8vo. 5s. net.
> New York: Macmillan & Co.
> THE PRINCE'S QUEST AND OTHER POEMS. With a Bibliographical Note added. Second Edition. Fcap. 8vo. 4s. 6d. net.

WATT (FRANCIS).
> THE LAW'S LUMBER ROOM. Fcap. 8vo. 3s. 6d. net.
> [*In preparation.*

WATTS (THEODORE).
> POEMS. Crown 8vo. 5s. net. [*In preparation.*
> *There will also be an* Edition de Luxe *of this volume printed at the Kelmscott Press.*

WELLS (H. G.).
> SELECT CONVERSATIONS WITH AN UNCLE, SINCE DECEASED. With a Title-page designed by F. H. TOWNSEND. Fcap. 8vo. 3s. 6d. net.
> New York: The Merriam Co.

WHARTON (H. T.).
> SAPPHO. Memoir, Text, Selected Renderings, and a Literal Translation by HENRY THORNTON WHARTON. With three Illustrations in photogravure, and a Cover designed by AUBREY BEARDSLEY. Fcap. 8vo. 7s. 6d. net.
> Chicago: A. C. M'Clurg & Co.

THE YELLOW BOOK
An Illustrated Quarterly

Vol. I. Fourth Edition, 272 *pages,* 15 *Illustrations, Title-page, and a Cover Design. Cloth. Price* 5s. *net. Pott* 4to.

The Literary Contributions by MAX BEERBOHM, A. C. BENSON, HUBERT CRACKANTHORPE, ELLA D'ARCY, JOHN DAVIDSON, GEORGE EGERTON, RICHARD GARNETT, EDMUND GOSSE, HENRY HARLAND, JOHN OLIVER HOBBES, HENRY JAMES, RICHARD LE GALLIENNE, GEORGE MOORE, GEORGE SAINTSBURY, FRED. M. SIMPSON, ARTHUR SYMONS, WILLIAM WATSON, ARTHUR WAUGH.

The Art Contributions by Sir FREDERIC LEIGHTON, P.R.A., AUBREY BEARDSLEY, R. ANNING BELL, CHARLES W. FURSE, LAURENCE HOUSMAN, J. T. NETTLESHIP, JOSEPH PENNELL, WILL ROTHENSTEIN, WALTER SICKERT.

Vol. II. Third Edition. Pott 4to, 364 pages, 23 Illustrations, and a New Title-page and Cover Design. Cloth. Price 5s. net.

The Literary Contributions by FREDERICK GREENWOOD, ELLA D'ARCY, CHARLES WILLEBY, JOHN DAVIDSON, HENRY HARLAND, DOLLIE RADFORD, CHARLOTTE M. MEW, AUSTIN DOBSON, V., O., C. S., KATHARINE DE MATTOS, PHILIP GILBERT HAMERTON, RONALD CAMPBELL MACFIE, DAUPHIN MEUNIER, KENNETH GRAHAME, NORMAN GALE, NETTA SYRETT, HUBERT CRACKANTHORPE, ALFRED HAYES, MAX BEERBOHM, WILLIAM WATSON, and HENRY JAMES.

The Art Contributions by WALTER CRANE, A. S. HARTRICK, AUBREY BEARDSLEY, ALFRED THORNTON, P. WILSON STEER, JOHN S. SARGENT, A.R.A., SYDNEY ADAMSON, WALTER SICKERT, W. BROWN MACDOUGAL, E. J. SULLIVAN, FRANCIS FORSTER, BERNHARD SICKERT, and AYMER VALLANCE.

A Special Feature of Volume II. is a frank criticism of the Literature and Art of Volume I. by PHILIP GILBERT HAMERTON.

Vol. III. Third Edition. Now Ready. Pott 4to, 280 pages, 15 Illustrations, and a New Title-page and Cover Design. Cloth. Price 5s. net.

The Literary Contributions by WILLIAM WATSON, KENNETH GRAHAME, ARTHUR SYMONS, ELLA D'ARCY, JOSÉ MARIA DE HÉRÉDIA, ELLEN M. CLERKE, HENRY HARLAND, THEO MARZIALS, ERNEST DOWSON, THEODORE WRATISLAW, ARTHUR MOORE, OLIVE CUSTANCE, LIONEL JOHNSON, ANNIE MACDONELL, C. S., NORA HOPPER, S. CORNISH WATKINS, HUBERT CRACKANTHORPE, MORTON FULLERTON, LEILA MACDONALD, C. W. DALMON, MAX BEERBOHM, and JOHN DAVIDSON.

The Art Contributions by PHILIP BROUGHTON, GEORGE THOMSON, AUBREY BEARDSLEY, ALBERT FOSCHTER, WALTER SICKERT, P. WILSON STEER, WILLIAM HYDE, and MAX BEERBOHM.

THE PUBLICATIONS OF JOHN LANE

Vol. IV. Second Edition. Now Ready. Pott 4to, 285 pages, 16 Full-page Illustrations. With New Title-page and Cover Designs and a Double-page Supplement by Aubrey Beardsley. Price 5s. net.

The Literary Contributions by RICHARD LE GALLIENNE, HENRY HARLAND, GRAHAM R. TOMSON, H. B. MARRIOTT WATSON, DOLF WYLLARDE, MÉNIE MURIEL DOWIE, OLIVE CUSTANCE, JAMES ASHCROFT NOBLE, LEILA MACDONALD, C. S., RICHARD GARNETT, VICTORIA CROSS, CHARLES SYDNEY, KENNETH GRAHAME, C. NEWTON ROBINSON, NORMAN HAPGOOD, E. NESBIT, MARION HEPWORTH DIXON, C. W. DALMON, EVELYN SHARP, MAX BEERBOHM, and JOHN DAVIDSON.

The Art Contributions by H. J. DRAPER, WILLIAM HYDE, WALTER SICKERT, PATTEN WILSON, W. W. RUSSELL, A. S. HARTRICK, CHARLES CONDER, WILL ROTHENSTEIN, MISS SUMNER, P. WILSON STEER, and AUBREY BEARDSLEY.

Vol. V. Now Ready. Pott 4to, 317 pages, 16 Full-page Illustrations and New Title-page and Cover Designs. Price 5s. net.

The Literary Contributions by WILLIAM WATSON, H. D. TRAILL, RICHARD LE GALLIENNE, ELLA D'ARCY, ROSAMUND MARRIOTT-WATSON, KENNETH GRAHAME, HENRY HARLAND, DAUPHIN MEUNIER, MRS. MURRAY HICKSON, EDMUND GOSSE, CHARLES KENNETT BURROW, LEILA MACDONALD, HUBERT CRACKANTHORPE, ERNEST WENTWORTH, C. S., G. S. STREET, NORA HOPPER, JAMES ASHCROFT NOBLE, B. PAUL NEUMAN, EVELYN SHARP, W. A. MACKENZIE, MRS. ERNEST LEVERSON, RICHARD GARNETT, MAURICE BARING, NORMAN GALE, ANATOLE FRANCE, and JOHN DAVIDSON.

The Art Contributions by E. A. WALTON, R. ANNING BELL, ALFRED THORNTON, F. G. COTMAN, P. WILSON STEER, A. S. HARTRICK, ROBERT HALLS, WALTER SICKERT, CONSTANTIN GUYS, SYDNEY ADAMSON, and PATTEN WILSON.

Prospectuses Post Free on Application.

LONDON : JOHN LANE
BOSTON : COPELAND & DAY

www.ingramcontent.com/pod-product-compliance
Lightning Source LLC
Chambersburg PA
CBHW020905230426
43666CB00008B/1321